MAINE
IN THE AGE
OF DISCOVERY

Christopher Levett's Voyage, 1623-1624
and
A Guide to Sources

Maine Historical Society

1988

Preface

Christopher Levett's account of his voyage to New England in 1623-24 was reprinted in 1847, in Volume II, *Collections of the Maine Historical Society*. It is reprinted here in corrected form, drawn from the original edition of 1624 in the collections of the British Library. Levett's charming account is of interest to students of history, natural history, and anthropolgy. It is preceded by an introduction by Roger Howell, Jr., William R. Kenan, Jr. Professor of Humanities at Bowdoin College and President of the Maine Historical Society. His essay explores the impetus for English voyages in the Elizabethan Age, Levett's life, the values implicit in English colonization, and the goals of publishing the account in 1624.

The account is followed by a guide to sources on Maine in the age of discovery, compiled and annotated by Emerson W. Baker, II, Executive Director of the York Institute Museum—Dyer Library. Here the casual reader and scholar alike are introduced to the secondary sources for the study of prehistoric archeology, the many voyages to the Maine coast, early British and French colonization, and Indian-European relations.

Levett's "Voyage into New England" and its companion pieces have been published to complement the "Land of Norumbega: Maine in the Age of Exploration and Settlement," a major project of the Maine Humanities Council. To the Council and its staff go our appreciation for their encouragement and support of this publication.

The Maine Historical Society gathers, makes available, and interprets evidence of Maine's rich heritage. Our commitment to education and research, for both scholars and amateurs, has inspired a publications program that is as old as the Society itself. It is with pride that we invite the reader to use our resources to undertake a personal exploration of Maine and its history.

Elizabeth J. Miller
Executive Director, Maine Historical Society

Roger Howell, Jr. is a graduate of Bowdoin College and Oxford University. A member of the Bowdoin faculty since 1964, he was formerly a Research Fellow and Dean of St. John's College, Oxford. He is a specialist in Tudor-Stuart history and is the author of seven books and numerous articles on the period. He is currently President of the New England Historical Association and is a member of the Council of the North American Conference on British Studies.

Emerson W. Baker has worked for the Dyer Library and York Institute Museum in Saco, Maine since 1986, first as historian and archaeologist, and currently as executive director. He holds a B.A. from Bates College, an M.A. from the University of Maine, and a Ph.D. in history from the College of William and Mary. He is the author of *The Clarke & Lake Company: The Historical Archaeology of a Seventeenth-Century Maine Settlement*, as well as several articles on the history and archaeology of early colonial Maine.

Table of Contents

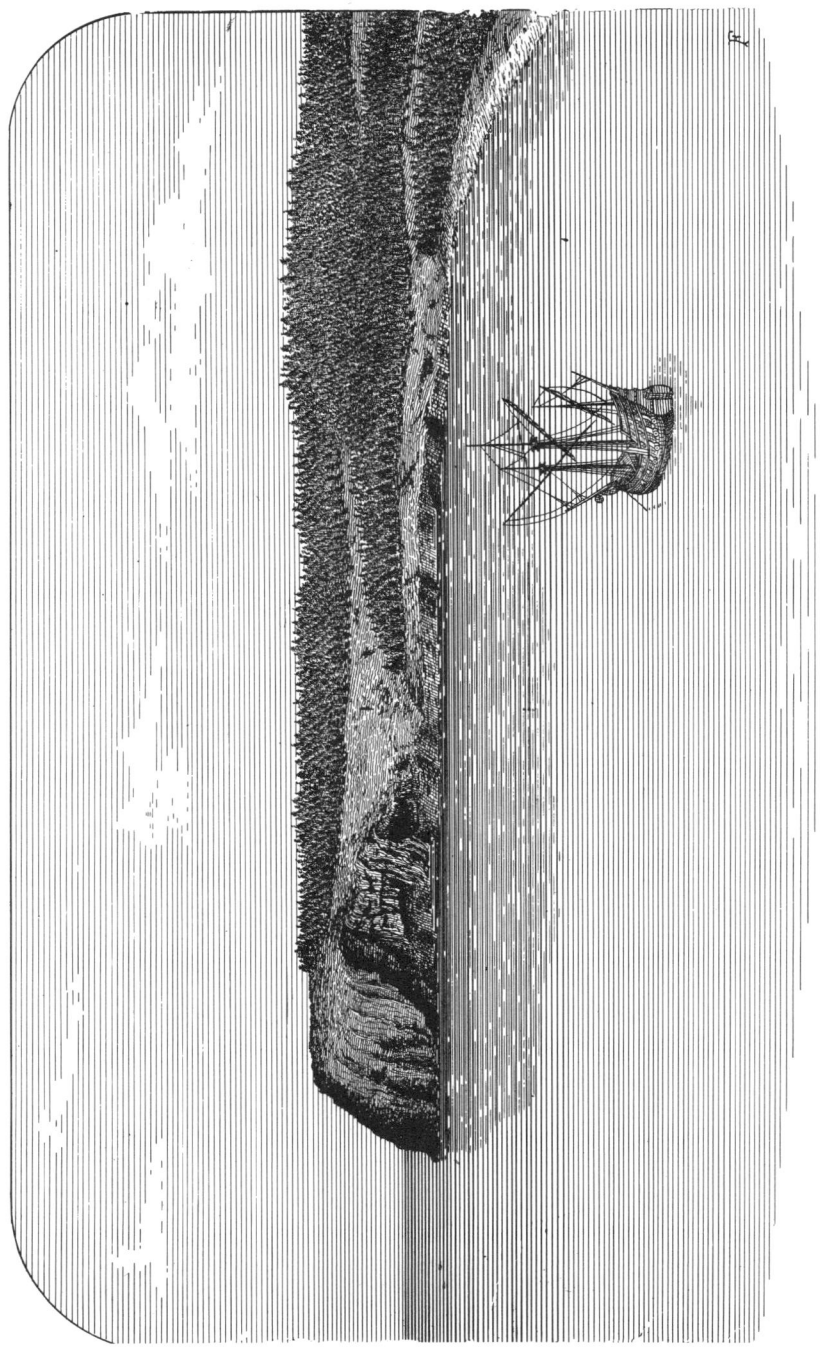

CAP^{T} LEVETT AT ANCHOR IN WHITE-HEAD COVE AUG. 1623.

Introduction

BY

Roger Howell, Jr.

Christopher Levett's voyage to the coast of Maine in 1623-1624 occurred at a significant but embattled moment in the history of English exploration and projected colonization in New England. Because of this, it has a dual interest. On the one hand, it contains a vivid narrative of his adventures and observations; through his recollections, the modern reader is able to gain some appreciation of how the New World appeared to a seventeenth century Englishman, what features attracted his notice, how he reacted to the natives, what significance he placed on that which was revealed to him. On the other hand, Levett's account is plainly part of the promotional literature designed to popularize the idea of New England colonization and draw both financial backers and potential settlers to the cause. Its composition, initial publication, and later reissue were all initimately connected with the fortunes of the Council for New England, the chartered organization created by Sir Ferdinando Gorges to further his schemes for settlement in New England. Levett's account, viewed in this regard, is more than just a travel narrative; it is an argument advancing the reasons why settlement in New England would be beneficial to the English commonwealth. Thus, it provides valuable insight into English as well as New England history and offers some indications of the motives that led to exploration and projected settlement in the 1620s. The date is significant; Levett's account pre-dates the ascendancy of the Laudian church in England and the so-called Great Migration. Although religious considerations were probably never very far from the mind of a seventeenth-century Englishman, Levett was writing before the settlement of New England had cloaked itself substantially in the mantle of a religious exodus, and the reasons he advances for supporting the settlement scheme were designed to appeal more to those who kept a close tally of their accounts than to those who did so of their spiritual blessings and earthly transgressions.

I: LEVETT'S ENGLAND

The England in which Levett was born in the spring of 1586 was, in many ways, a society of contradictions. Posterity has bestowed on the long reign of Elizabeth I a vitality, confidence, and stability which are more illusory than real. The great age of voyaging and discovery had indeed begun and doubtless the exploits of Drake, Hawkins, Raleigh, Grenville, and Frobisher stirred the imaginations of many. Propagandists of empire had already advanced the case for imperial expansion, urging reasons ranging from profit to power, from the duty of converting the heathen to the cultivation of the quality of *virtu* in those who took part.[1] Yet England in the 1580s was also a beleaguered nation and very conscious of that fact. Dwarfed in size and resources by the rival monarchies of France and Spain, it was painfully on the defensive against what it saw as the menace of international Catholicism.[2] While a coterie of Protestant activists argued that the country should take a more aggressive stance by forming a Protestant league and by carving out an empire that would simultaneously strategically damage the Catholic powers, enrich the mother country, solve its pressing social problems of poverty and perceived over-population, and serve the glory of God,[3] the political leadership of the country was realistically more cautious. Queen Elizabeth and her great advisor, William Cecil, Lord Burghley, were acutely aware of England's limitations and its precarious position. Caution and balance were their watchwords, rather than aggression and dominance.[4] They encouraged the more lively spirits only when it suited their purposes and did not unduly touch their pockets; otherwise, they sought to keep them in check. Even the East India Company found the granting of its charter delayed for a year because Elizabeth felt that its creation might undo her diplomatic relations with Spain.

Despite the lukewarm and somewhat reluctant attitude of the crown, efforts at stimulating interest in the colonial enterprise went on, and during the years that Levett grew to manhood a sizeable literature developed and, alongside it, some sobering experience with respect to New England had been accumulated. English familiarity with New England had its roots in the Elizabethan period and was increased, albeit spasmodically in the following reign of James I.[5] If English fishermen were the first to make use of New England landfalls, they were joined towards the end of Elizabeth's reign by men of a quite different stamp. Influenced by the writings of imperial publicists like Dr. John Dee and the Hakluyts,[6] mariners began to explore the eastern coastline of America with a view to finding favorable locations for the establishment of colonies. Such voyagers included men like Bartholomew Gosnold and John Brereton who spent part of the summer of 1602 on Martha's Vineyard, Martin Pring who coasted from Maine to Cape Cod in the following year, and George Waymouth who explored the Kennebec River in 1605. Anxious to stimulate interest and more directly to gain financial backing, these early travellers had a considerable tendency to paint an over-favorable image of what they had seen. A picture emerged of a land of extraordinary abundance, ripe for the taking and teeming with natural resources ranging from timber to mineral deposits simply waiting for the English to profit from them. In part this was sheer puffery, in part wishful thinking, in part plain ignorance occasioned by the experience of summer voyaging. But all in all, it added up to a very favorable press.

Against this pleasant picture of a land of untold promise, there was set the much more unfavorable impression derived from actual experience of attempted settlement in New England, notably the failure of the settlement at Sagadahoc.[7] Launched with great enthusiasm by Sir Ferdinando Gorges and Sir John Popham in 1607, it had been abandoned within a year of its foundation. In retrospect, this effort can be seen to have been badly organized and full of false expectations, such as the hope of finding extensive deposits of precious metal. The severity of the winter came as a profound and unexpected shock and far from being the desirable location they had expected, New England turned out to be, in their estimation, "a cold, barren, mountainous, rocky desert."[8] Those who survived the experience were all too quick to tell those who would listen that New England held no promise after all, a point that those who were anxious to stimulate interest in colonization further south were ready to second. There can be little doubt that the circulation of such negative reports by word of mouth did much to retard interest in New England settlement in the early years of James I's reign. Nor did the favorable reports of Captain John Smith, who travelled to New England in 1614, or the continuing enthusiasm of Sir Ferdinando Gorges for a New England venture entirely offset them. In the second decade of the seventeenth century, those Englishmen who had any impression of New England at all had before their eyes an incomplete, muddled and often contradictory picture.

II: CHRISTOPHER LEVETT AND NEW ENGAND

Of the early life of Christopher Levett, which occurred during these years, there is little to be gleaned.[9] He was born, as has been noted, in 1586 in the city of York, one of four children of Percival and Elizabeth Levett. His father was an innkeeper but nonetheless a man of some substance in the city; he had become a freeman in 1581 and had held city office, serving as Chamberlain in 1584 and Sheriff in 1597-8. His mother was related to the gentry of the surrounding countryside and had inherited property from her uncle, Robert Rotherforth. No details survive of Christopher's education; he tended to play it down, referring to himself at a later date as "but a young scholar though an ancient traveller by sea,"[10] but his own literary output suggests that he had an adequate training in letters and there is, in addition, evidence that the Levett family put an emphasis on education.[11] Information about his early livelihood is equally shadowy. Apparently he turned to the sea to seek a living; he later noted, "I have no calling to employ myself in not being bred up to anything but the sea and in that neither no otherwise than a traveller and commander of some merchant ships."[12] He continued, however, to live in York. In 1608, he married Mercy, the daughter of Robert More, the Puritan rector of Guisley. Four children were born to this marriage between 1610 and 1614; all the children were baptized in the city of York, indicating Levett's continuing residence there.

His wife Mercy died sometime shortly after the birth of the fourth child, and at this time a significant change came over the career of Levett. Leaving his native city of York, for which he retained a strong affection, he moved to Sherborne in the county of Dorset. Here he contracted a second and favorable marriage to Frances Lottisham, the daughter of Oliver Lottisham of Farrington, Somerset. Since the Lottishams were an established county family of some standing, the marriage can probably be seen as evidence of Levett's upward social mobility. Two further children came of this marriage in 1615 and 1619. Apparently the couple lived in relative comfort; Levett was to remark a few years later, "I thank God I have sufficient to maintain me in a reasonable good fashion."[13] By means that are not entirely clear, Levett was also acquiring powerful friends, most notably the Duke of Buckingham. He found employment in the royal forests as the king's woodward in Somerset; his duties included protecting the timber against illegal depredations and selecting trees suitable for masts. If, as he claimed, Levett performed his duties conscientiously, he was something of an exception to the prevailing norm in the local forest administration; the leading historian of the subject sadly commented that "such police duty was ineffectively performed, for most of the offices declined into nominal positions, often without pay and with a consequent neglect of duty."[14] Drawing on his experience, though, Levett composed a short tract in 1618, *An Abstract of Timber Measures,* "drawn into a brief method by way of arithmetic and contrived into such a form that the most simple man in the world, if he do but know figures in their places, may understand it, and by the due observing of it, shall be made able to buy and sell with any man, be he never so skillful, without danger of being deceived."[15] The book was, with optimism and no doubt an eye to possible future favor, dedicated to King James himself.

It was apparently at about this time that Levett's thoughts began to turn to the New World. The orientation is hardly surprising, given the fact that the west country was the source of much early English interest in New England. Taking up the cause of New England settlement had something of the aura of a spiritual conversion to Levett. Writing in 1624 he recalled:[16]

About five or six years since, it pleased God to open my eyes that I see plainly that my youth was spent in vanity and that my course of life was no way pleasing to him (though I could not be much taxed by any), and that I must take a new course if I meant to live forever with Christ in his kingdom. Ever since, I have earnestly desired that God in mercy could use me as an instrument to bring glory to his name and some good to his church and this commonwealth wherein I live; when the first motion for New England was made unto me, I took council of some reverend and worthy friends who advised me to it by all means.

From whence came "the first motion" and who the friends were does not appear, but inexorably this new orientation led to involvement in the work of the Council for New England and the aspirations of Sir Ferdinando Gorges.

The Council for New England had been incorporated on 3 November 1620 under the name of the Council established at Plymouth in the County of Devon, for the planting, ruling, ordering and governing of New England in America. It was substantially a reincorporation of the earlier Adventurers of the

Northern Colony of Virginia, and Gorges remained its ruling spirit.[17] From the very outset, the newly chartered corporation faced a tide of criticism from the Virginia Company, from fishing interests who resented its power to grant licenses to fish on the coast, and from a growing body of opinion in the House of Commons which resisted the spread of monopolies. Gorges counted on the power of the court and court associates to secure his ventures against such criticism. The list of patentees reads, as one author put it, "like an abstract from the peerage."[18] Support of this sort was far from negligible; when a complaint against the Council for New England, lodged by the Virginia Company, was heard before the Privy Council, a number of those hearing the complaint were sitting in their own case, and in such a setting Gorges had little trouble in holding his own. Parliamentary opposition was more difficult to control; successive adjournments of Parliament held up the attack, but hostility to Gorges and the Council for New England grew, while support fell away; "all men were afraid to join with us," Gorges sadly noted.[19] The problems of the Council, in fact, ran even deeper; it operated on the slimmest of financial resources. While the original patentees may have been useful to the Council as friends at court, they were noticeably less forthcoming in their role as financial backers. As Dr. Rowse has observed, "the New England Council simply never had enough resources; it lived from hand to mouth."[20]

It was this financial situation which enabled Levett, already contemplating a New England venture, to entwine his affairs with those of the Council. On 5 May 1623, he became a principal patentee on the payment of £110 and a grant was made to him of 6000 acres of land, to be selected by him within the limits of his charter.[21] Levett himself, however, still needed financial backing to further his ambitions, and this he hoped to raise by an appeal to his native city of York. His principal bait to lure such backing was his proposal "to build a city and call it by the name of York."[22] Levett was able to enlist some powerful support behind this scheme. Secretary Conway, along with Buckingham one of the most influential men at Court, was able to persuade the King himself to stand behind Levett's proposal, and he wrote a letter in June to that effect to further Levett's appeal.[23]

His suit is that he might have adventurers to join with him to set forth fifty men with fifty others that he intends to carry over and that such as shall be unwilling to adventure may nevertheless be moved to contribute towards building of a fort which he intends to make for the preservation of those that are to depend upon him and to secure the plantation. His majesty's request therefore to your Lordship is that you will employ your industry and your judicious mediation between the gentlemen of that county and Mr. Levett and by all fair persuasions to wean from the county some assistance upon such conditions as may be just and suitable with his reputation, which favor his majesty will acknowledge as done at his request.

While support did not apparently materialize on the scale Levett hoped for, he was able to obtain a ship and sufficient men. His departure for New England must have taken place within a relatively short space of time after Conway's appeal.

Levett provided no account of his Atlantic crossing. The details of the voyage he "conceived to be impertinent...to relate" and he feared that he would "not only be tedious, but also be in danger of losing myself, for want of fit phrases and sound judgment in the arts of the mathematics and navigation."[24] He made landfall at the Isles of Shoals sometime in the autumn of 1623. These he found of little attraction, noting there were no good timber trees nor sufficient good ground to make a garden and that the harbor was at best indifferent. He then proceeded to Pannaway (Odiorne's Point near the mouth of the Piscataqua) where David Thompson, an agent of Gorges, had shortly before established a small settlement. There he remained for a month, gathering his men who had arrived in other vessels and surveying as much as he possibly could, though he noted this was complicated by unseasonable weather and much snow. It was while he was staying with Thompson that he discovered for the first time that he was even more closely involved in the affairs of the Council for New England than he had imagined. Gorges had sent over his son Robert as Governor and Lieutenant General of New England, accompanied by Captain Francis West, bearing the title of Admiral of New England and the Reverend William Morrell, who was to see to church affairs. This attempt to make the paper authority of the Council of New England a reality was to prove futile on every level, but Levett was now joined directly with it, being sworn a member of Robert Gorge's council.[25]

Bolstered with this new authority and with the season already well advanced, Levett and his men ventured eastward along the coast in two open boats. In the vicinity of York harbor (Aquamenticus), he found an area which he thought good for a plantation, there being a good harbor, good timber, and good ground, already cleared and fit for planting as a result of prior Indian occupation. The next harbor he noted was at Cape Porpoise; sufficient for six ships, it held out excellent promise for fishing and since there was abundant timber and suitable ground, it might also prove to be a good plantation, though Levett cautioned that it would involve considerable labor and charge to develop.

As Levett proceeded eastwards, the hazards and the inconveniences of his undertaking became increasingly evident. Between Cape Porpoise and what he designated as Saco (which would seem to be Fletcher's Neck and Biddeford Pool), one of his men was lost under circumstances he did not relate. Before reaching the harbor, his boats were caught in a heavy fog, separated from one another and then exposed to a fierce storm. After a harrowing night at sea, the boats were reunited, but his exploring was then held up for a further five days by contrary winds. Buffetted by rain and snow, his company built crude shelters with the sails of the ship. Though cheered by the availability of good fresh water and ample fowl to supply their diet, the men were obviously living in most uncomfortable surroundings. Levett put a good face on it all and even claimed that the spreading of long dry grass in the shelter had produced a degree of comfort. Thwarted by the wind, Levett explored on foot the area of what is now Old Orchard Beach. In the end, he fell sick, doubtless, as he surmised, as a result of the wet and the cold coupled with high levels of physical exertion. His speedy recovery was a tribute to a robust constitution.

The wind having changed, Levett once again put to sea and reached the place called Quack which he renamed York. He described it as a bay between the mainland and certain islands, with a good harbor being formed by the four islands. What he described in general terms was quite clearly Portland harbor and the western part of Casco Bay. He found the area much to his liking with good fishing, abundant game, and ground as good as a man could desire. In the Fore River, which he christened with his own name, he was told by the Indians there were many salmon. He likewise explored up the Presumpscot River till he was halted by the falls.

Levett continued his exploration further eastward. The whole of the region between Cape Elizabeth and Sagadahoc he deemed to be highly desirable for plantations. Of Sagadahoc itself he related nothing, other than that two ships had fished there during the year. The consciousness of the failure of the earlier colony and the dampening effect that had had on colonial enterprise was clearly in his mind. "Of Sagadahoc, I need say nothing of it; there hath been heretofore enough said by others, and I fear too much."[26] He proceeded eastward to what he called Capemanwagan, which can be identified with Southport or possibly Boothbay Harbor. Here he lingered for four days, meeting with a number of Indians and indulging in some trade with them. Levett had apparently intended to continue further east but changed his mind, in part because the Indians told him that there was no good place to be found there, in part because he knew of grants to other Englishmen, but in the main because he had already decided to establish himself at Quack which he had renamed York. That determination was further strengthened by the fact that Cogawesco, the Sagamore of Casco and Quack had indicated that he would be pleased to have Levett settle in either of those areas.

His return to Casco Bay must have been an impressive sight for he brought Cogawesco and his immediate family with him in his boat with Cogawesco's companions alongside in their canoes. The return was both auspicious and inauspicious. In almost matter of fact fashion, Levett recorded how, after "many dangers, much labour, and great charge"[27] he had obtained a place of habitation and had proceeded to build a house and fortify it in good fashion. Where Levett's house actually was is a matter of conjecture. All that is known is that it was on an island that was later described as "lying before Casco [Fore] River." House Island fits the description and may well be the spot, but the matter cannot now be definitely resolved.[28] If the friendly attitude of the Indians, his favorable reception by the fishermen operating in the area, and the construction of his fortified house were the positive aspects of the picture, a negative aspect soon surfaced as well in the form of a direct challenge to the very authority from which Levett held his claim. The master of one of the vessels in the harbor was aggressively trading with the Indians; not content just to cut into Levett's profits, he also sought to break down Levett's good relations with the Indians. Levett found that his grant from the Council for New England and his position as a councillor under Robert Gorges made little or no impact on this captain, whom he could only regard as an impertinent interloper. His adversary simply replied that he acknowledged no authority in that place and that he intended to trade even though he was forbidden to do so; his "warrant" was simply one of force, for he had what Levett described as "a great ship,"[29] armed with seventeen pieces of ordnance and fifty men. Levett was quite right to point out to the Council for New England that if they let such action go unanswered, they would have no authority over anyone in those parts. But the truth was that the Council already had no real authority in the area, as the failure of Robert Gorges' mission had shown. Levett was simply experiencing in Casco Bay a personal example of a general problem.

Sometime in the summer of 1624, having completed his house and fortifications, Levett sailed for home. He left behind ten of his men to look after his interests in Casco Bay and he departed with the evident good will of the Indian community, who expressed a keen desire for his speedy return. If the affairs of the Council for New England had been precarious when Levett had sailed from England, they were more so now on his return. Levett needed to solicit further support in men and money if his project was to go forward, but the discouraging report on affairs in New England brought back by Robert Gorges had hardly served to create a favorable climate for this. It is little wonder that one of the first things Levett did on his return was to pen his account of his travels and add to it all the arguments he could muster in support of the colonial exterprise. The tract was published at the end of August 1624 by William Jones, who had also published his earlier *Abstract of Timber Measures.*[30]

If Levett had hoped that his pamphlet would lead to a surge of support for his New England scheme, he was to be disappointed. The ensuing years were clearly ones of considerable frustration on his part. The Council for New England was decidedly on the defensive and his association with it became more of a liability than an advantage. Under vigorous attack in parliament as a monopoly, it could do little to guarantee his title to his grant, and without that security, Levett had little prospect of securing the additional men and money that he required. As early as December 1624, Levett was chafing under his circumstances. Writing to Secretary Coke the day after Christmas, he still asserted his confidence that the New England scheme could be a success, but sought in the meantime some other form of employment since he found his enforced idleness unendurable. "I am persuaded if I may have some assistance, I should bring that to pass which I so much thirst after" he wrote, but then continued, "help me forwards with that or some other employment, for truly as I now live my life is a burden to me....it is even a death to me to live idle."[31] While Coke could not immediately provide any support for the New England enterprise, he was able eventually to provide some alternate employment for Levett in October 1625 when Levett was made captain of the *Susan and Ellen* and sailed in her as part of the disastrous naval expedition to Cadiz.[32]

The Cadiz expedition could have brought little satisfaction in itself to Levett, but its aftermath opened up an important channel for him. Probably at the suggestion of Secretary Coke, Levett penned an extended account of what he had observed on the expedition and significantly used it as a vehicle for once again bringing to the attention of the Secretary the cause of New England. A settlement there, he argued, could become a vital part of an overall strategy to strike at the power of Spain. Levett's proposal was as bold as it was simplistic. First, he recommended that all trade with Spain be halted and that the navy be used to cut off Spanish trade with Hamburg and Dunkirk. Then the English fishing places in New England and Newfoundland should be fortified "or otherwise it is to be feared we shall lose a more profitable country than the West Indies."[33] All this, Levett argued, could be done at a modest cost of one subsidy; "in consideration of that one charge our nation shall forever receive from thence such a yearly profit as shall maintain a reasonable army or fleet or maintain all the poor."[34] Relief of the poor would, in his view, cease to be a problem within a period of twenty years "except for blind, lame, and old people that shall not be able to work;"[35] presumably he felt that the able-bodied poor would be attracted to New England by the opportunities there and thus relieve England of its most pressing domestic social problem. In addition, he postulated that New England itself, once it had been fortified, would be able to supply a ship of five hundred tons a year. The end result would be that "they shall be able to do more hurt to the King of Spain and his West Indies than all England."[36] Levett expressed his desire to appear before parliament or the Council to elaborate further on his views and to show that they were reasonable. Recognizing that the proposal might seem too good to be true, Levett urged on Coke his own qualifications and specialist knowledge: "I assure you that when I was in the country of New England I took more pains (though to my cost) to find out the nature of the country, the disposition of the inhabitants, and the commodities which was there to be had, as also the best means to obtain them than any man that was in the country, and I dare say further than any that ever was there before me."[37] While Levett clearly had a personal interest in such attention being paid to New England, he disavowed any desire for personal gain and argued that he only sought that which was best for the Commonwealth; "If I can bring glory to God, honor to my sovereign, and good to my native country, then shall I think myself more happy than if I had the whole world."[38]

There was no quick response to Levett's proposals. At the end of November 1626, Levett again wrote to Coke pushing his ideas:[39]

Your Honor knows what opinions I have of New England and my grounds for the same, and I must need say the more I think of it, the more I affect it. There is no man knows better than myself what benefit would accrue unto this kingdom by that country if it were well planted and fortified, which makes me so desirous to tread out a path that all men may follow.

I am now in a fair way to it, only I want a little help to further me....the particulars I have mentioned in a petition to his majesty....I fly unto your your Honor as my only mediator unto his majesty for the obtaining of my request.

That response was slow is hardly surprising. The Court was much distracted by other concerns, such as Buckingham's ill-fated expedition to La Rochelle. Levett continued to propagandize for his plan. In October 1627 he wrote an additional letter to Coke, enclosing this time a letter from one of his servants in New England, presumably one of the men he had left behind at his fort in Casco Bay; his purpose was to reiterate his concern about the speedy settling of the affairs of New England and the fortification of settlements there:[40]

I know as well how to make that country good against an enemy as any subject his Majesty hath, and can do it with a tenth part of the charge that another shall demand, nay with no charge at all in comparison if a fit time be taken....I beseech your Honor, let not the multiplicity of weighty and chargeable affairs which are now in hand cause this to be neglected, for I assure you if it be not speedily put in execution, much damage and dishonor must certainly ensue.

On Buckingham's return from his expedition to La Rochelle, he passed through Sherborne, where Levett had again taken up residence, and Levett was able to press the New England project on him, as he reported in a letter to Coke in November. With the letter he included a more detailed summary of his intended actions in New England.[41] He argued that the period of greatest danger was the time between the beginning of June and the end of January; during those months, the fishing fleet was absent, but the fishermen would have left their shallops behind in various harbors, thus providing an easy means of transportation for an enemy. Levett's proposal was that all the shallops be collected together in a single harbor, and he suggested his own settlement of York as the most suitable for that purpose. York would then be fortified by four ships, and an attempt would be made to draw all the planters to that location; if that proved not to be feasible, the planters outside of York should be provided arms and ammunition for their defense. Levett urged that there be a speedy dispatch of the ships, arguing that since they would thus be there during the fishing season, the charges of the voyage might well be defrayed and the other fishermen who were present could provide additional labor to work on the fortifications. Whether it was because of Coke's efforts, the support of Buckingham, or the sheer persistence of Levett, the scheme this time received a favorable hearing from the King and Council. The upshot was the issue of a remarkable proclamation by the King enjoining the ecclesiastical authorities to take up a collection in the various churches of the country on behalf of Levett's enterprise in Casco Bay. The wording of the proclamation echoed the repeated appeals of Levett, both with regard to the importance of the undertaking and to the suitability of Levett himself to direct the enterprise:[42]

Whereas our many urgent occasions do at this present so far engage us for the necessary defense of this our realms and dominions as we cannot in due time give any assistance or provide for the securing of those remote parts with such succour and relief as may prove requisite, in a case of that importance, whereby that plantation so happily begun and likely to prove so advantageous and profitable to us and our subjects, in regard of the many commodities and merchandise thence to be had, and the store of timber there growing, very necessary for the provision of shipping for the defense of our kingdoms is likely to be utterly lost and abandoned, to the dishonor of us and our nation and the advantage and encouragement of our enemies; and whereas we have been informed that our well-beloved subject Captain Christopher Levett, being one of the Council for the said plantation, and well knowing the said country and the harbors of the same, and the strength and disposition of the Indians inhabiting in that country, hath undertaken and offered to add unto his former adventure there all his estate, and to go in person thither, and by God's assistance either to secure the planters from enemies, keep the possession of the said country on our behalf, and secure the fishing for our English ships, or else to expose his life and means to the uttermost pill in that service, upon which his generous and free offer we have thought fit, by the advice of our Privy Council, and appointed him to be Governor for us in those parts.

In directing the churches to take up a collection to support Levett, the King stressed an argument which, while not absent from Levett's own case, was not the main thrust of it, namely "the propagation of the true religion which by this means may be affected, by converting those ignorant people to Christianity."[43]

No evidence survives to indicate what success was achieved by this royal directive. Levett himself did his best to publicize his cause by having his 1624 pamphlet reissued. In all probability, the returns on this appeal were negligible. The mood of the country by 1628 was hardly favorable to additional royal levies, even if they were voluntary, especially if the levies were for schemes backed by Buckingham. In addition, many of those who would have been most inclined to respond to the anti-Spanish thrusts of Levett's arguments were not only highly suspicious of the religious policy of the government but were also increasingly inclined to think that a Caribbean venture, rather than a New England one, would be the most effective way to strike at Spain.[44]

At some point after June 1628, Levett did indeed return to New England.[45] Whether he ever returned to Casco Bay is unknown. Certainly he had disposed of his interest in the settlement before his death, selling his patent to several Plymouth merchants.[46] But he was in Salem in 1630; John Winthrop recorded that when he cast anchor there on 12 June,

"Mr. Pierce came aboard us and returned to fetch Mr. Endicott, who came to us about two of the clock, and with him Mr. Skelton and Captain Levett."[47] It is the last glimpse of Levett alive; he was in command of a ship that shortly afterwards sailed for England. He died on the voyage home and was buried at sea. On January 1631, the probate records of Bristol recorded that his widow had travelled there from Sherborne to claim his personal affects.[48]

III: LEVETT'S WORLD OF IDEAS

In discussing Levett's ideas, it is important to avoid a possible misapprehension. Christopher Levett was in no way, as he himself was at pains to point out, a systematic thinker. He was an educated and articulate adventurer, a mariner, and a practical-minded promoter of colonial schemes. At the same time, though, he was a perceptive observer and, in his zeal to promote settlement in the New World, he was, by the very nature of things, compelled to express ideas about the physical reality of New England, its inhabitants, and the reasons why Englishmen should undertake a hazardous sea voyage to settle there. Christopher Levett's world of ideas was inevitably much affected by the general climate of opinion in early Stuart England. Thus, some of what he said was hardly unique; similar comments could have been and were penned by a number of his contemporaries. But there were also, at times, comments of a quite personal and individual nature.

One of the most obvious and important concerns for Levett was to convey to his fellow Englishmen a vivid sense of the territory concerned. A dominant theme in his presentation was the need to be both accurate and realistic in that description. Levett was well aware of the fact that the credibility of much of the early promotion literature had been called into question by actual experience. Hence he was at pains to tell his readers that he was not writing a description of a false paradise where nature rewarded the settler without any effort on the settler's part:[49]

I will not do therein as some have done, to my knowledge speak more than is true:I will not tell you that you may smell the corn-fields before you see the land, neither must men think that corn doth grow naturally (or on trees), nor will the deer come when they are called, or stand still and look on a man until he shoot him, not knowing a man from a beast; nor the fish leap into the kettle, nor on the dry land, neither are they so plentiful that you may dip them up in baskets, nor take cod in nets to make a voyage, which is no truer than that the fowls will present themselves to you with spits through them.

Levett, in fact, was careful to include in his account some of the inconveniences of the territory; in particular, he pointed to mosquitoes in the summer and snow in the winter. To be sure, he went on to argue that such inconveniences could be overcome; such statements are to be expected in a tract designed to encourage settlement. Proper clothing and smoke from fires would minimize the mosquito problem, and he expressed the hope that the clearing of the land by settlement would further reduce the difficulty. He was perhaps unduly sanguine with respect to the problems caused by snow. Modern day natives of the area may well be amused by the assertion that it does not snow until Christmas and that the cold period is of no great duration. Levett also stressed a simple, if misleading geographical fact, which reveals the limits of his knowledge of the factors affecting climate. Since New England was further from the North Pole than England, it should, he asserted, also be hotter.

Levett's account of New England, and in particular of the Casco Bay region in which he was personally interested, is predictably enthusiastic. It is important to note what he did stress. There were ample supplies of game and fish for the taking, though he carefully qualified that observation by noting that settlers would have to be diligent in the taking of them. There was good meadow, pasture and arable land. Given his own maritime background and the needs of his country, it is not surprising that Levett placed the greatest stress on naval-related resources such as good harbors and ample supplies of timber for planks and masts. All that was lacking, to his mind, was iron, but he thought that deficiency could easily be remedied, since iron could be imported as ballast in incoming shipping.

With respect to the native Indians, Levett had, on the whole, a tolerant view. Despite the fact that he consistently referred to them as savages and was critical of their religion, which he felt was tinged with witchcraft, he strongly urged that the Indians should be accorded fair treatment and that efforts should be made to live peacefully with them, though he was careful to add a caution that the settlers should not trust them too far:[50]

They are very bloody-minded and full of treachery amongst themselves; one will kill another for their wives, and he that hath the most wives is the bravest fellow; therefore I would wish no man to trust them, whatever they say or do; but always to keep a strict hand over them, and yet to use them kindly, and deal uprightly with them; so shall they please God, keep their reputation amongst them, and be free from danger.

Two observations on the Indians made by Levett appear particularly striking. The first concerns their wives. Levett's terse comment that their wives were their slaves and did all their work is expressed with an indignation that is all the more telling given the inferior status of women in his own contemporary England.[51] Even more striking, though, is his observation that the Indians have rights in their land which should be respected by the settlers. Though he admitted that he had made a resolution to settle in the Casco Bay area, Levett stressed the importance of the fact that the local sagamore had given him permission to do so; he was, he noted, "glad of this opportunity, that I had obtained the consent of them, who as I conceive hath a natural right of inheritance, as they are the sons of Noah."[52]

If Levett felt that the Indians should be treated fairly, he also insisted that colonization would serve positive purposes for England and that it should be pursued aggressively. The reasons he advanced in favor of vigorous activity in this regard were, for the most part, commonplaces that would have been familiar to many seventeenth century Englishmen. He was willing to admit that there had been failures among earlier colonizing efforts, yet he suggested that lack of success was more the product of individual failing than it was of anything inherently wrong about the New World. He repeatedly emphasized the point that while wealth and resources were there for the taking, the manner of the taking was crucial; forethought, careful planning and hard work were all essential. No one should expect to profit or even survive without labor; Levett warned families against migrating to the colonies unless they had one laborer for every three non-laborers in the family unit. Likewise, no one should contemplate a voyage unless he had eighteen months' provision, so that he could take advantage of two seasons in the colony before his initial provision was expended. But if people were willing to labor and if they made adequate preparations, then the potential benefits to the commonwealth were, in Levett's view, substantial. Colonization would, he felt, increase the trade, wealth, and prosperity of England. This he saw as a good in itself but also as important for the country's place in international relations. Menaced by the Catholic powers of France and Spain, England with the aid of New England colonization would be strengthened in its resistance. Moreover, colonization was presented as a solution to England's social problems. Levett shared in the common perception that England was overpopulated; the New England colonies would provide a vital safety-value in this regard. Likewise, they would to his mind provide a solution to the pressing problem of the poor that increasingly concerned the English upper classes. Emigration of the able-bodied poor would convert a social problem into an economic asset, while the profits derived from the colonial venture would provide funds to relieve the burden of the poor rates for the impotent poor who remained at home.

Levett's own arguments for colonization were primarily economic, political, and social in nature. He did not make much of the religious argument, although that figured prominently in the proclamation of Charles I which was designed to raise funds for his endeavors. In fact, Levett stated that he had at best limited hopes for the conversion of the Indians. "I have had much conference with the savages about our only true God, and have done my best to bring them to know and acknowledge him; but I fear all the labor that way will be lost, and no good will be done, except it be among the younger sort."[53] For all that pessimism, Levett appears to have been a man of strong religious faith. When threatened by a storm at sea off Saco, Levett turned to prayer, albeit only after prudently setting his anchor; in harrowing conditions on land, he noted that his greatest comfort was spiritual.[54] Elsewhere, he refers to the condition of him and his men as being "much better than we deserved at God's hands, if he should deal with us according to our sins" and, when he was arguing that colonization was the answer to England's poverty, he pointedly commented, "if we will endure poverty in England wilfully, and suffer so good a country as this is to lie waste, I am persuaded we are guilty of a grievous sin against God, and shall never be able to answer it."[55] It is possible, though by no means certain, that Levett was inclined towards Puritanism, even if he did not make much of religion in his arguments. Two facts would seem to point in that direction. His first father-in-law, Robert More, was certainly of a Puritan temperament, and on the voyage home during which he died Levett was carrying letters that were critical of the established church and its government;[56] while it is possible that he was unaware of their contents, the conjunction is suggestive.

When Levett wrote of his conversion to the idea of a New England venture, he used language that was strongly reminiscent of a Puritan describing his spiritual conversion. While it certainly would be too strong to suggest that concern with the New World became his religion, that interest clearly dominated the latter stages of his life. In the end, his schemes came to naught, and there is a certain appropriateness in the fact that this rugged mariner died at sea somewhere between his two worlds of England and New England. What he left to posterity was not a flourishing settlement in Casco Bay but rather an enthralling account of how he struggled to make that settlement a reality. His monument is not the city of York he hoped to found to honor his birthplace but a pamplet that richly illumines the lure of Stuart voyaging to New England.

A Note on the Present Edition

The text that has been employed here is that of the original 1624 edition and the subsequent reprint of 1628. The two texts are identical except for the title page. The previous reprints in the *Collections of the Maine Historical Society* and in James P. Baxter, *Christopher Levett of York* were both unaware of the 1624 edition; the latter is a more accurate transcription than the former. The spelling has been modernized throughout, with the exception of personal and place names and a few technical terms. Numbers have been written out, although they do not always appear in this form in the original. In the main, the original punctuation has been adhered to, though it has occasionally been amended for the sake of clarity. The usage of capitals and italics has followed modern practice rather than the somewhat more haphazard employment prevalent in the seventeenth century. A handful of textual emendations have been made where the sense appeared to require it; the most significant are indicated by brackets in the text. It will be noted that there is no chapter four in the text, despite the title provided for it in the table of contents; it has been elided with chapter three as the result of a printer's error, although the transition from the description of the Indians to the description of the country, which marks its beginning, is obvious. The error was probably the result of the haste with which the 1624 edition was prepared, but it was not corrected in the 1628 reprint. Levett's account has been left to speak for itself, unencumbered by a host of explanatory footnotes. Most of the places he describes are readily identifiable and the persons he mentions traceable in standard reference works if they are not at once familiar. In any case, the introduction serves to provide the context for his account and further annotation would seem superfluous.

REFERENCES

1. On such literature see H. M. Jones, "The Colonial Impulse: An Analysis of the 'Promotion' Literature of Colonization, " *Proceedings of the American Philosophical Society,* vol. 90 (1946), pp. 131-161.

2. On the perception of the Catholic threat, see C. Z. Wiener, "The Beleaguered Isle: A Study of Elizabethan and Early Jacobean Anti-Catholicism," *Past and Present,* no. 51 (1971), pp. 27-62.

3. R. Howell, "The Sidney Circle and the Protestant Cause in Elizabethan Foreign Policy, "*Renaissance and Modern Studies,* vol. 19 (1975), pp. 31-46.

4. R. B. Wernham, *Before the Armada: The Growth of English Foreign Policy 1485-1588* (London, 1966); R. B. Wernham, *The Making of Elizabethan Foreign Policy 1558-1603* (Berkeley, 1980).

5. A. L. Rowse, *The Elizabethans and America* (London, 1959).

6. On Dee see W. I. Trattner, "God and Expansion in Elizabethan England: John Dee, "*Journal of the History of Ideas,* vol. 25 (1964), pp. 17-34; on Richard Hakluyt, see G. B. Parks, *Richard Hakluyt and the English Voyagers* (New York, 1928).

7. On the Sagadahoc experiment, see C. M. Andrews, *The Colonial Period of American History* (New Haven, 1934), 1: 78-97.

8. D. Cressy, *Coming Over: Migration and Communication between England and New England in the Seventeenth Century* (Cambridge, 1987), p. 3.

9. The fullest account of the life of Levett, on which I have drawn heavily, is J. P. Baxter, *Christopher Levett of York, the Pioneer Colonist in Casco Bay* (Portland, 1893).

10. See below, p. 35.

11. His nephew John was also an author and his son Jeremy was a graduate of Cambridge and became a preacher. Baxter, *Christopher Levett,* p. 4.

12. Christopher Levett to Sir John Coke, 26 December, 1624, printed *ibid.* p. 29.

13. *Ibid.*

14. R. G. Albion, *Forests and Sea Power: the Timber Problem of the Royal Navy 1652-1862* (reprint edition, Hamden, 1965), p. 109.

15. C. Levett, *An Abstract of Timber Measures* (London, 1618).

16. Christopher Levett to Sir John Coke, 26 December, 1624, printed in Baxter, *Christopher Levett,* p. 28.

17. On Gorges and the organization of the New England colonial enterprise, see Andrews, *Colonial Period*, 1: chap. 16; Rowse, *Elizabethans and America*, chap. 5; and R. A. Preston, *Gorges of Plymouth Fort* (Toronto, 1953). The records of the Council for New England were printed in *Proceedings of the American Antiquarian Society*, no. 47 (1867), pp. 53-96, supplemented by a further selection printed *ibid*, no. 65 (1875) pp. 49-63 and then paginated to run on consecutively from the pagination of no. 47, as pp. 96(2)-131.

18. C. F. Adams, *Three Episodes in Massachusetts History* (Boston, 1892), 1: 122.

19. Rowse, *Elizabethans and America*, p.106.

20. *Ibid.*, p. 105.

21. *Proceedings of the American Antiquarian Society*, no. 47 (1867), p. 94.

22. Secretary Conway to the Lord President of York, 26 June 1623, printed in Baxter, *Christopher Levett*, p. 14.

23. *Ibid.*

24. See below, p. 35.

25. On Robert Gorges' mission see Andrews, *Colonial Period,* I: 338-43; Rowse, *Elizabethans and America*, pp. 110-111, and Preston, *Gorges,* pp. 226-229. William Bradford summed up the situation when he noted that Gorges "and some that depended upon him returned to England, having scarcely saluted the country in his government, not finding the state of things here to answer his quality and condition." W. Bradford, *Of Plymouth Plantation 1620-1647*, ed. S. E. Morison (New York, 1962), p. 138.

26. See below, p. 44.

27. See below, p. 46.

28. On the location of his fort, see Baxter, *Christopher Levett*, pp. 105-107, note 56.

29. See below, p. 48.

30. The title page of the 1624 edition gives the date of publication as August 21.

31. Christopher Levett to Sir John Coke, 26 December 1624 printed in Baxter, *Christopher Levett*, pp. 28-29.

32. On the Cadiz expedition, see C. Carlton, *Charles I: The Personal Monarch* (London, 1983), pp. 73-77.

33. "Captain Levett's Relation," printed in Baxter, *Christopher Levett*, p. 51.

34. *Ibid.*, p. 52.

35. *Ibid.*

36. *Ibid.*

37. *Ibid.*, p. 53.

38. *Ibid.*

39. Christopher Levett to Sir John Coke, 29 November 1626, printed *Ibid.*, pp. 58-9.

40. Christopher Levett to Sir John Coke, 10 October 1627, printed *Ibid.*, p. 62.

41. Christopher Levett to Sir John Coke, 17 November 1627, printed *Ibid.*, pp. 63-66.

42. Proclamation of Charles I, 11 February 1628, printed *Ibid.*, pp. 68-9.

43. *Ibid.*, p. 69.

44. K. O. Kupperman, "Errand to the Indies: Puritan Colonization from Providence Island through the Western Design," *William and Mary Quarterly*, 3rd. series, vol. 45 (1988), pp. 70-99.

45. Since he was concerned with agitation in the House of Commons over a monopoly of his uncle to collect tolls on two bridges in Doncaster until June, it is unlikely he left before then. See Baxter, *Christopher Levett*, pp. 72-73.

46. H. S. Burrage, *The Beginnings of Colonial Maine 1602-1658* (Portland, 1914), pp. 225-6.

47. J. Winthrop, *The History of New England from 1630 to 1649* (Boston, 1853), 1:30.

48. Baxter, *Christopher Levett*, p. 76.

49. See below, pp. 54-55.

50. See below, p. 53.

51. On the status of women in seventeenth century England, see A. Fraser, *The Weaker Vessel: Woman's Lot in Seventeenth-Century England* (London, 1984).

52. See below, p. 45.

53. See below, p. 52.

54. See below, p. 40.

55. See below, pp. 41, 67.

56. Winthrop, *History of New England*, 1: 119.

A
VOYAGE
INTO NEVV
ENGLAND

Begun in 1 6 2 3. and ended
in 1 6 2 4.

Performed by CHRISTOPHER LEVETT,
his Maiesties Woodward of *Somerset-shire*, and
one of the Councell of New-England.

Yorkes  Bonauen-
ture.

Printed at LONDON, by WILLIAM IONES,
and are to be sold by *Edward Brewster*, at the signe
of the Bible in Paules Church yard.
1628.

To the Right Honorable, George Duke of Buckingham, his Grace, Thomas Earl of Arundell and Surrey, Robert Earl of Warwick, John Earl of Holderness, and the rest of the Council for New England.

May it please your Lordships, that whereas you granted your commission unto Captain Robert Gorges, Governor of New England, Captain Francis West, myself, and the Governor of New Plymouth, as counsellors with him, for the ordering and governing of all the said territories, wherein we have been diligent to the uttermost of our powers, as we shall be ready to render an account unto your honors, when you shall be pleased to require us thereunto. In the mean time, I thought it my duty to present unto your views, such observation as I have taken, both of the country and people, commodities and discommodities: as also, what places are fit to settle plantations in, in which not; what courses are fit in my understanding to be taken, for bringing glory to God, honor to our king and nation, good unto the commonwealth, and profit to all adventurers and planters; which I humbly beseech your lordships to accept of, as the best fruits of a shallow capacity: so shall I think my time and charge well employed, which I have spent in these affairs.

I have omitted many things in this my discourse, which I conceived to be impertinent at this time for me to relate, as of the time of my being at sea, of the strange fish which we there saw, some with wings flying above the water, others with manes, ears, and heads, and chasing one another with open mouths like stone horses in a park, as also of the steering of our course, the observation of the sun and stars, by which the elevation of the pole is found, the degrees of latitude known, which shows how far a ship is out of his due course, either to the north or south; likewise of the making of the land at our arrival upon the coast of New England, how it did arise and appear unto us; how every harbor bears one from another upon the point of the compass; and what rocks and dangers are in the way; how many fathom water is found by sounding at the entrance of every harbor; and from how many of the several winds all the harbors are land-locked. But by this means I thought I should not only be tedious, but also be in danger of losing myself, for want of fit phrases and sound judgment, in the arts of the mathematics and navigation, (being but a young scholar though an ancient traveller by sea,) and therefore thought better to omit those, than anything I have to relate.

Thus beseeching God to bless your Honors, I rest at your Lordships' service.

Christopher Levett

The Contents

Contains my discovery of divers Rivers and Harbors, with their names, and which are fit for plantations, and which not.

The first place I set my foot upon in New England, was the Isle of Shoulds, being islands in the sea, about two leagues from the main.

Upon these islands, I neither could see one good timber tree, nor so much good ground as to make a garden.

The place is found to be a good fishing place for six ships, but more cannot well be there, for want of convenient stage room, as this year's experience hath proved.

The harbor is but indifferent good. Upon these islands are no savages at all.

The next place I came unto was Pannaway, where one M. Tomson hath made a plantation, there I stayed about one month, in which time I sent for my men from the east: who came over in divers ships.

At this place I met with the Governor, who came thither in a bark which he had from one M. Weston about twenty days before I arrived in the land.

The Governor then told me that I was joined with him in commission as a counsellor, which being read I found it was so. And he then, in the presence of three more of the council, administered unto me an oath.

After the meeting of my men, I went a coasting in two boats with all my company.

In the time I stayed with M. Tomson, I surveyed as much as possible I could, the weather being unseasonable, and very much snow.

In those parts I saw much good timber, but the ground it seemed to me not to be good, being very rocky and full of trees and brushwood.

There is a great store of fowl of divers sorts, whereof I fed very plentifully.

About two English miles further to the east, I found a great river and a good harbor called Pascattaway. But for the ground I can say nothing, but by the relation of the sagamore or king of that place, who told me there was much good ground up in the river about seven or eight leagues.

About two leagues further to the east is another great river called Aquamenticus. There I think a good plantation may be settled, for there is a good harbor for ships, good ground, and much already cleared, fit for planting of corn and other fruits, having heretofore been planted by the savages who are all dead. There is good timber, and likely to be good fishing, but as yet there hath been no trial made that I can hear of.

About six leagues further to the east is a harbor called Cape Porpas, the which is indifferent good for six ships, and it is generally thought to be an excellent place for fish, but as yet there hath been no trial made, but there may be a good plantation seated, for there is good timber and good ground, but will require some labor and charge.

About four leagues further east, there is another harbor called Sawco (between this place and Cape Porpas I lost one of my men); before we could recover the harbor a great fog or mist took us that we could not see a hundred yards from us. I perceiving the fog to come upon the sea, called for a compass and set the cape land, by which we knew how to steer our course, which was no sooner done but we lost sight of land, and my other boat, and the wind blew fresh against us, so that we were enforced to strike sail, and betake us to our oars which we used with all the wit and strength we had, but by no means could we recover the shore that night, being imbayed and compassed round with breaches, which roared in a most fearful manner on every side [of] us: we took counsel in this extremity one of another what to do to save our lives; at length we resolved that to put to sea again in the night was no fit course, the storm being great, and the wind blowing right off the shore, and to run our boat on the shore amongst the breaches, (which roared in a most fearful manner) and cast her away and endanger ourselves we were loath to do, seeing no land nor knowing where we were. At length I caused our killick (which was all the anchor we had) to be cast forth, and one continually to hold his hand upon the rood or cable, by which we knew whether our anchor held or no: which being done we commended ourselves to God by prayer, and put on a resolution to be as comfortable as we could, and so fell to our victuals. Thus we spent that night, and the next morning, with much ado we got into Sawco, where I found my other boat.

There I stayed five nights, the wind being contrary, and the weather very unseasonable, having much rain and snow, and continual fogs.

We built us our wigwam, or house, in one hour's space. It had no frame, but was without form or fashion, only a few poles set up together, and covered with our boats' sails, which kept forth but a little wind, and less rain and snow.

Our greatest comfort we had, next unto that which was spiritual, was this: we had fowl enough for killing, wood enough for felling, and good fresh water enough for drinking. But our beds was the wet ground, and our bedding our wet clothes. We had plenty of crane, goose, ducks and mallard, with other fowl, both boiled and roasted, but our spits and racks were many times in danger of burning before the meat was ready (being but wooden ones.)

After I had stayed there three days, and no likelihood of a good wind to carry us further, I took with me six of my men, and our arms, and walked along the shore to discover as much by land as I could: after I had travelled about two English miles I met with a river which stayed me that I could go no further by land that day, but returned to our place of habitation where we rested that night (having our lodging amended); for the day being dry I caused all my company to accompany me to a marsh ground, where we gathered every man his burthen of long dry grass, which being spread in our wigwam or house, I praise God I rested as contentedly as ever I did in all my life. And then came into my mind an old merry saying, which I have heard of a beggar boy, who said if ever he should attain to be a king, he would have a breast of mutton with a pudding in it, and lodge every night up to the ears in dry straw; and thus I made myself and my company as merry as I could, with this and some other conceits, making this use of all, that it was much better than we deserved at God's hands, if he should deal with us according to our sins.

The next morning I caused four of my men to row my lesser boat to this river, who with much ado got in, myself and three more going by land; but by reason of the extremity of the weather we were enforced to stay there that night, and were constrained to sleep upon the river bank, being the best place we could find, the snow being very deep. The next morning we were enforced to rise betime, for the tide came up so high that it washed away our fire, and would have served us so too if we had not kept watch. So we went over the river in our boat, where I caused some to stay with her, myself being desirous to discover further by land, I took with me four men and walked along the shore about six English miles further to the east, where I found another river, which stayed me. So we returned back to Sawco, where the rest of my company and my other boat lay. That night I was exceeding sick, by reason of the wet and cold and much toiling of my body: but thanks be to God I was indifferent well the next morning, and the wind being fair we put to sea, and that day came to Quack.

But before I speak of this place I must say something of Sawco, and the two rivers which I discoverd in that bay, which I think never Englishman saw before.

Sawco is about one league to the north-east of a cape land. And about one English mile from the main lieth six islands, which make an indifferent good harbor. And in the main there is a cove or gut, which is about a cable's length in breadth, and two cable's length long, there two good ships may ride, being well moored ahead and stern; and within the cove there is a great marsh, where at a high water a hundred sail of ships may float, and be free from all winds, but at low water must lie aground, but being soft ooze they can take no hurt.

In this place there is a world of fowl, much good timber, and a great quantity of clear ground and good, if it be not a little too sandy. There hath been more fish taken within two leagues of this place this year than in any other in the land.

The river next to Sawco eastwards, which I discovered by land, and after brought my boat into, is the strangest river that ever my eyes beheld. It flows at the least ten foot water upright, and yet the ebb runs so strong that the tide doth not stem it. At three quarters flood my men were scarce able with four oars to row ahead. And more than that, at full sea I dipped my hand in the water, quite without the mouth of the river, in the very main ocean, and it was as fresh as though it had been taken from the head of a spring.

This river, as I am told by the savages, cometh from a great mountain called the Chrystal hill, being as they say one hundred miles in the country, yet is it to be seen at the sea side, and there is no ship arrives in New England, either to the west so far as Cape Cod, or to the east so far as Monhiggen, but they see this mountain the first land, if the weather be clear.

The next river eastward which I discovered by land, is about six miles from the other. About these two rivers I saw much good timber and sandy ground, there is also much fowl, fish and other commodities: but these places are not fit for plantation for the present, because there is no good coming in either for ship or boat, by reason of a sandy breach which lieth alongst the shore, and makes all one breach.

And now in its place I come to Quack, which I have named York. At this place there fished divers ships of Waymouth this year.

It lieth about two leagues to the east of Cape Elizabeth. It is a bay or sound betwixt the main and certain islands which lieth in the sea about one English mile and half.

There are four islands which makes one good harbor; there is very good fishing, much fowl, and the main as good ground as any can desire. There I found one river wherein the savages say there is much salmon and other good fish. In this bay there hath been taken this year four sturgeons, by fishermen who drive only for herrings, so that it is likely there may be good store taken if there were men fit for that purpose. This river I made bold to call by my own name, Levett's river, being the first that discovered it. How far this river is navigable I cannot tell; I have been but six miles up it, but on both sides is goodly ground.

In the same bay I found another river, up which I went about three miles, and found a great fall of water, much bigger than the fall at London bridge at low water; further a boat cannot go, but above the fall the river runs smooth again.

Just at this fall of water the sagamore or king of that place hath a house, where I was one day when there were two sagamores more, their wives and children, in all about fifty, and we were but seven. They bid me welcome and gave me such victuals as they had, and I gave them tobacco and aqua vitae. After I had spent a little time with them I departed and gave them a small shot, and they gave me another. And the great Sagamore of the east country, whom the rest do acknowledge to be chief amongst them, he gave unto me a beaver's skin, which I thankfully received, and so in great love we parted. On both sides this river there is goodly ground.

From this harbor to Sagadahock, which is about eight or nine leagues, is all broken islands in the sea, which makes many excellent good harbors, where a thousand sail of ships may ride in safety; the sound going up within the islands to the cape of Sagadahock. In the way betwixt York and Sagadahock lieth Cascoe, a good harbor, good fishing, good ground, and much fowl. And I am persuaded that from Cape Elizabeth to Sagadahock, which is above thirty leagues to follow the main, is all exceeding commodious for plantations; and that there may be twenty good towns well seated, to take the benefit both of the sea, and fresh rivers.

For Sagadahock I need say nothing of it, there hath been heretofore enough said by others, and I fear me too much. But the place is good; there fished this year two ships.

The next place I came to was Capemanwagan, a place where nine ships fished this year. But I like it not for a plantation, for I could see little good timber and less good ground; there I stayed four nights, in which time there came many savages with their wives and children, and some of good account amongst them, as Menawormet, a sagamore, Cogawesco, the sagamore of Casco and Quack, now called York, Somerset, a sagamore, one that hath been found very faithful to the English, and hath saved the lives of many of our nation, some from starving, others from killing.

They intended to have been gone presently, but hearing of my being there, they desired to see me, which I understood by one of the masters of the ships, who likewise told me that they had some store of beaver coats and skins, and was going to Pemaquid to truck with one Mr. Witheridge, a master of a ship of Bastable, and desired me to use means that they should not carry them out of the harbor. I wished them to bring all their truck to one Mr. Coke's stage, and I would do the best I could to put it away: some of them did accordingly, and I then sent for the sagamores, who came, and after some compliments they told me I must be their cousin, and that Captain Gorges was so, (which you may imagine I was not a little proud of, to be adopted cousin to so many great kings at one instant, but did willingly accept of it) and so passing away a little time very pleasantly, they desired to be gone, whereupon I told them that I understood they had some coats and beaver skins which I desired to truck for: but they were unwilling, and I seemed careless of it (as men must do if they desire anything of them.) But at last Somerset swore that there should be none carried out of the harbor, but his cousin Levett should have all; and then they began to offer me some by way of gift, but I would take none but one pair of sleeves from Cogawesco, but told them it was not the fashion of English captains always to be taking, but sometimes to take and give, and continually to truck was very good. But in fine, we had all except one coat and two skins, which they reserved to pay an old debt with; but they staying all that night, had them stolen from them.

In the morning the sagamores came to me with a grievous complaint. I used the best language I could to give them content, and went with them to some stages which they most suspected, and searched both cabins and chests, but found none. They seeing my willingness to find the thief out, gave me thanks, and wished me to forbear, saying the rogues had carried them into the woods where I could not find them.

When they were ready to depart they asked me where I meant to settle my plantation. I told them I had seen many places to the west, and intended to go farther to the east before I could resolve; they said there was no good place, and I had heard that Pemoquid, and Capmanwagan, and Monhiggon were granted to others, and the best time for fishing was then at hand, which made me the more willing to retire, and the rather because Cogawesco, the sagamore of Casco and Quack, told me if that I would sit down at either of those two places, I should be very welcome, and that he and his wife would go along with me in my boat to see them; which courtesy I had no reason to refuse, because I had set up my resolution before to settle my plantation at Quack, which I named York, and was glad of this opportunity, that I had obtained the consent of them, who as I conceive hath a natural right of inheritance, as they are the sons of Noah, and therefore do think it fit to carry things very fairly without compulsion, (if it be possible) for avoiding of treachery.

The next day the wind came fair, and I sailed to Quack or York, with the king, queen, and prince, bow and arrows, dog and kettle in my boat, his noble attendance rowing by us in their canoes.

When we came to York the masters of the ships came to bid me welcome, and asked what savages those were. I told them, and I thanked them; they used them kindly, and gave them meat, drink, and tobacco. The woman or reputed queen, asked me if those men were my friends. I told her they were; then she drank to them, and told them they were welcome to her country, and so should all my friends be at any time; she drank also to her husband, and bid him welcome to her country too; for you must understand that her father was the sagamore of this place, and left it to her at his death, having no more children.

And thus after many dangers, much labor and great charge, I have obtained a place of habitation in New England, where I have built a house, and fortified it in a reasonable good fashion, strong enough against such enemies as are those savage people.

Sheweth how the Savages carried themselves unto me continually, and of my going to their Kings' houses; and their coming to mine.

Whilst I stayed in this place I had some little truck, but not much, by reason of an evil member in the harbor, who being covetous of truck used the matter so that he got the savages away from me.

And it is no wonder he should abuse me in this sort, for he hath not spared your lordships and all the council for New England.

He said unto the governor that the lords had sent men over into that country with commissions, to make a prey of others. And yet for my own part I never demanded or took from any man in that country, the value of a denier, neither had I so much help from any ship or ship's company as one man's labor the space of an hour, nor had I any provision or victual upon any terms whatsoever, save only one thousand of bread, and twenty-two bushels of peas, which was offered unto me, and not by me requested, for which I gave present satisfaction in beaver skins: and also one runlet of aqua vitae, which was brought to me sixteen leagues unexpected, which good manners bid me buy. Much more provision was offered to me by many masters of ships, but I had no need thereof, so I gave them thanks for their kindness, and refused all.

Nay, it is well known, that I was so far from doing wrong to any, that I suffered the land which was granted to me by patent, and made choice of before any other man came there, to be used, and my timber to be cut down and spoiled, without taking or asking any satisfaction for the same. And I doubt not but all others to whom you gave authority, will sufficiently clear themselves of all such imputations.

He said also he cared not for any authority in that place, and though he was forbid to truck, yet would he have all he could get: in despite of who should say to the contrary, having a great ship with seventeen pieces of ordnance and fifty men.

And indeed his practice was according to his words, for every Sunday, or once in the week, he went himself or sent a boat up the river and got all the truck before they could come down to the harbor. And so many savages as he could get to his stage, he would enforce them to leave their goods behind them. One instance amongst many I will give you.

On a certain day there came two savages to his place, who were under the command of Somerset or Conway, I know not whether, at which time they were both with me at my house, but the other two who went to him, knew not so much, but afterwards they understanding of it, came presently over, but left their coats and beaver skins behind them, whereat Somerset and Conway were exceeding angry; and were ready to beat the poor fellows, but I would not suffer them so to do. They presently went over the harbor themselves in their canoe to fetch their goods, but this man would let them have none, but wished them to truck with him; they told him they would not, but would carry them to Captain Levett; he said Levett was no captain, but a jacknape, a poor fellow, &c. They told him again that he was a rogue, with some other speeches, whereupon he and his company fell upon them and beat them both, in so much that they came to me in a great rage against him, and said they would be revenged on his fishermen at sea, and much ado I had to dissuade one of them for going into England to tell king James of it, as he said; when they came to me in this rage, there was two or three masters of ships by, and heard every word.

But all this did me no hurt, (save the loss of the truck, which by divers was thought to be worth about fifty pounds,) for the two sagamores whom he enticed from me and incensed against me, at length used means to be friends with me, sending one who asked me, if I were angry with them; I told them no, I was not angry with them for any such matter as lousy coats and skins, but if they were *matchett,* that is naughty men, and rebellious, then I would be *mouchick hoggery,* that is very angry, and would *cram,* that is kill them all.

When they came themselves to me to seek peace, they brought me a beaver coat, and two otter skins, which they would have let me had for nothing, but I would not take them so, but gave them more than usually I did by way of truck. I then told them likewise that if at any time they did truck with me, they should have many good things in lieu of their beaver; and if they did not truck it was no matter, I would be good friends with them; at which they smiled and talked one to the other, saying the other man was a jacknape, and that I had the right fashion of the *aberieney* sagamores; then they began to applaud or rather flatter me, saying I was so big a sagamore, yea four fathom, which were the best words they could use to express their minds: I replied that I was a poor man as he had reported of me. They said again it was no matter what I said, or that jacknape (which is the most disgraceful word that may be in their conceit,) for all the sagamores in the country loved poor Levett and was *muchicke* sorry that he would be gone, and indeed I cannot tell what I should think of them, for ever after they would bring me anything they thought would give me content, as eggs and the whole bodies of beaver, which in my conceit eat like lamb, and is not inferior to it: yea the very coats of beaver and otter skins from off their backs, which though I many times refused, yet not always, but I never took any such courtesy from them, but I requited them answerably, choosing rather to neglect the present profit, than the hopes I have to bring them to better things, which I hope will be for a public good, and which I am persuaded were a grievous sin, to neglect for any sinister end.

And a little before my departure there came these sagamores to see me: Sadamoyt, the great sagamore of the east country, Manawormet, Opparunwit, Skedraguscett, Cogawesco, Somerset, Conway and others.

They asked me why I would be gone out of their country? I was glad to tell them my wife would not come thither except I did fetch her; they bid a pox on her hounds, (a phrase they have learned and do use when they do curse) and wished me to beat her. I told them no, for then our God would be angry. Then they run out upon her in evil terms, and wished me to let her alone and take another; I told them our God would be more angry for that. Again they bid me beat her, beat her, repeating it often, and very angerly, but I answered no, that was not the English fashion, and besides she was a good wife and I had children by her, and I loved her well, so I satisfied them. Then they told me that I and my wife and children, with all my friends, should be heartily welcome into that country at any time, yea a hundredth thousand times, yea *mouchicke, mouchicke,* which is a word of weight.

And Somerset told that his son (who was born whilst I was in the country, and whom he would needs have to name) and mine should be brothers and that there should be *mouchicke legamatch,* (that is friendship) betwixt them, until Tanto carried them to his wigwam, (that is until they died.)

Then they must know of me how long I would be wanting. I told them so many months, at which they seemed to be well pleased, but wished me to take heed I proved not *chechaske,* in that (that is, a liar.) They asked me what I would do with my house; I told them I would leave ten of my men there until I came again, and that they should kill all the Tarrantens they should see (being enemies to them) and with whom the English have no commerce. At which they rejoiced exceedingly, and then agreed amongst themselves that when the time should be expired, which I spoke of for my return, every one at the place where he lived would look to the sea, and when they did see a ship they would send to all the sagamores in the country, and tell them that poor Levett was come again. And thus instead of doing me hurt, I think that either he or I have done good to all planters, by winning their affections, (which may be made use of without trusting of them.)

But if your Lordships should put up this wrong done unto you, and the authority which you gave them, never expect to be obeyed in those parts, either by planters or fishermen; for some have not stuck to say, that if such a man, contemning authority, and abusing one of the council, and drawing his knife upon him at his own house, which he did, should go unpunished, then would not they care what they did hereafter.

And truly let me tell your Lordships, that if ever you intend to punish any for disobedience, or contempt of authority, this man is a fit instrument to make a precedent of for he is rich, and this year will gain the best part of five hundred pounds by that country, and he hath neither wife nor child, for whose sakes he should be spared.

And if he go free, as he hath domineered over us, to whom your Lordships gave authority, but no power to put it in execution, so will he grow unmannerly too with your Lordships, as he hath already begun.

And it will discourage men hereafter to take any authority upon them, or to go about to reform any abuses in those parts. And also it will hinder planters from going over, if fishermen be suffered not only to take away their truck, but also to animate the savages against them, for this is the way to cause all planters to have their throats cut.

But I leave these things to your Lordships' consideration, who have as well power as authority to punish such rebellious persons.

Thus having acquainted you with what I have done, seen, and heard, now give me leave to tell you what I think of the savages, the inhabitants of that country: as also to justify the innocent, I mean the country of New England, against the slanderous reports of this man, and some others, which I have heard, and likewise to deliver my opinion what courses I conceive to be most convenient to be taken, for bringing most glory to God, comfort, honor and benefit to our king, and our own native nation.

Sheweth the nature and disposition of the Savages, and of their several Gods, Squanto and Tanto.

I have had much conference with the savages about our only true God, and have done my best to bring them to know and acknowledge him; but I fear me all the labor that way will be lost, and no good will be done, except it be among the younger sort.

I find they have two gods: one they love and the other they hate: the god they love, they call Squanto, and to him they ascribe all their good fortunes.

The god they hate they call Tanto, and to him they ascribe all their evil fortunes, as thus, when any is killed, hurt or sick, or when it is evil weather, then they say, Tanto is *hoggry*, that is angry. When any dies, they say, Tanto carries them to his *wigwam*, that is his house, and they never see them more.

I have asked them where Squanto dwells; they say they cannot tell but up on high, and will point upwards. And for Tanto, they say far west, but they know not where.

I have asked them if at any time they have seen Squanto, or Tanto: they say no, there is none sees them but their pawwawes, nor they neither, but when they dream.

Their pawwawes are their physicians and surgeons, and as I verily believe they are all witches, for they foretell of ill weather, and many strange things; every sagamore hath one of them belongs to his company, and they are altogether directed by them.

On a time I was at a sagamore's house, and saw a martin's skin, and asked if he would truck it; the sagamore told me no: the pawwawe used to lay that under his head when he dreamed, and if he wanted that, he could do nothing: thus we may perceive how the devil deludes those poor people, and keeps them in blindness.

I find them generally to be marvellous quick of apprehension, and full of subtlety; they will quickly find any man's disposition, and flatter and humour him strangely if they hope to get anything of him; and yet will they count him a fool if he do not show a dislike of it, and will say one to another, that such a man is *mechecome.*

They are slow of speech, and if they hear a man speak much they will laugh at him, and say he is *mechecum,* that is a fool.

If men of place be too familiar with them, they will not respect them; therefore it is to be wished that all such persons should be wise in their carriage.

The sagamores will scarce speak to an ordinary man, but will point to their men, and say sanops must speak to sanops, and sagamores to sagamores.

They are very bloody-minded and full of treachery amongst themselves; one will kill another for their wives, and he that hath the most wives is the bravest fellow; therefore I would wish no man to trust them, whatever they say or do; but always to keep a strict hand over them, and yet to use them kindly, and deal uprightly with them; so shall they please God, keep their reputation amongst them, and be free from danger.

Their sagamores are no kings, as I verily believe, for I can see no government or law amongst them but club law; and they call all masters of ships sagamores, or any other man that they see have a command of men.

Their wives are their slaves, and do all their work; the men will do nothing but kill beasts, fish, &c.

On a time reasoning with one of their sagamores about their having so many wives, I told him it was no good fashion; he then asked me how many wives king James had; I told him he never had but one, and she was dead, at which he wondered, and asked me who then did all the king's work. You may imagine he thought their fashion was universal, and that no king had any to work for them but their wives.

They have no apparel but skins, except they have it from the English or French; in winter they wear the hair side inwards, in summer outwards. They have a piece of skin about their loins like a girdle, and between their legs goes another, made fast to the girdle before and behind, which serves to cover their nakedness; they are all thus apparelled, going bare-headed with long hair; sometimes you shall not know the men from the women but by their breasts; the men having no hair on their faces.

When their children are born they bind them on a piece of board, and set it upright, either against a tree or any other place. They keep them thus bound until they be three months old; and after, they are continuall naked until they be about five or six years. Ye shall have them many times take their children and bury them in the snow all but their faces for a time, to make them the better to endure cold; and when they are above two years old, they will take them and cast them into the sea, like a little dog or cat, to learn them to swim.

Their weapons are bows and arrows; I never saw more than two fowling pieces, one pistol, about four half-pikes, and three cutlasses amongst them, so that we need not to fear them much, if we avoid their treachery.

Their houses are built in half an hour's space, being only a few poles or boughs stuck in the ground and covered with the barks of trees.

Their language differs as English and Welsh. On a time the governor was at my house, and brought with him a savage, who lived not above seventy miles from the place which I have made choice of, who talking with another savage, they were glad to use broken English to express their mind each to the other, not being able to understand one another in their language.

And to say something of the country. I will not do therein as some have done to my knowledge, speak more than is true; I will not tell you that you may smell the corn-fields before you see the land; neither must men think that corn doth grow naturally, (or on trees,) nor will the deer come when they are called, or stand still and look on a man until he shoot him, not knowing a man from a beast; nor the fish leap into the kettle, nor on the dry land, neither are they so plentiful that you may dip them up in baskets, nor take cod in nets to make a voyage, which is no truer than that the fowls will present themselves to you with spits through them.

But certainly there is fowl, deer, and fish enough for the taking, if men be diligent; there be also vines, plum trees, cherry trees, strawberries, gooseberries, and rasps, walnuts, chestnut, and small nuts, of each great plenty; there is also great store of parsley, and divers other wholesome herbs, both for profit and pleasure, with great store of sassafras, sarsaparilla, and aniseeds.

And for the ground there is a large and goodly marsh to make meadow, higher land for pasture and corn.

There be these several sorts of earth, which I have seen, as clay, sand, gravel, yea, and as black fat earth, as ever I saw in England in all my life.

There are likewise these helps for ground, as seasand, oreworth or wrack, marl, blue and white, and some men say there is lime; but I must confess I never saw any limestone: but I have tried the shells of fish, and I find them to be good lime.

Now let any husbandman tell me whether there be any fear of having any kind of corn, having these several kinds of earth with these helps, the climate being full as good if not better than England.

I dare be bold to say also, there may be ships as conveniently built there as in any place of the world, where I have been, and better cheap. As for plank, crooked timber, and all other sorts whatsoever can be desired for such purpose, the world cannot afford better. Masts and yards of all sizes, there be also trees growing, whereof pitch and tar is made.

And for sails and all sorts of cordish you need not to want, if you but sow hemp and flaxseed, and after work it. Now there wants nothing but iron, and truly I think I have seen iron-stone there, but must acknowledge I have no great judgment in minerals, yet I have seen the iron-works in England, and this stone is like ours. But howsoever if the country will not afford iron, yet it may be easily brought, for it is good ballast for ships.

There is also much excellent timber for joiners and coopers; howsoever a worthy nobleman hath been abused, who sent over some to make pipe-staves; who either for want of skill or industry did no good. Yet I dare say no place in England can afford better timber for pipe-staves, than four several places which I have seen in that country.

Thus have I related unto you what I have seen, and do know may be had in those parts of New England where I have been, yet was I never at the Mesachusett, which is counted the paradise of New England, nor at Cape Ann. But I fear there hath been too fair a gloss set on Cape Ann. I am told there is a good harbor which makes a fair invitation, but when they are in, their entertainment is not answerable, for there is little good ground, and the ships which fished there this year, their boats went twenty miles to take their fish, and yet they were in great fear of making their voyages, as one of the masters confessed unto me who was at my house.

Neither was I at New Plymouth, but I fear that place is not so good as many others for if it were, in my conceit, they would content themselves with it and not seek for any other, having ten times so much ground as would serve ten times so many people as they have now amongst them. But it seems they have no fish to make benefit of, for this year they had one ship fish at Pemoquid, and another at Cape Ann, where they have begun a new plantation, but how long it will continue I know not.

Neither was I ever farther to the west than the Isle of Shoulds.

Thus have I done with my commendations of the country; I will now speak the worst I know by it.

About the middle of May you shall have little flies, called musketoes, which are like gnats; they continue, as I am told, until the last of July. These are very troublesome for the time, for they sting exceedingly both night and day. But I found by experience that boots or thick stockings would save the legs, gloves the hands, and tiffany or some such things which will not much hinder the sight, will save the face, and at night any smoke will secure a man.

The reason of the abundance of these creatures, I take to be the woods which hinders the air, for I have observed always when the wind did blow but a little, we were not much troubled with them.

And I verily think that if there were a good number of people planted together, and that the woods were cut down, the earth were tilled, and the rubbish which lieth on the ground wherein they breed were burnt, and that there were many chimneys smoking, such small creatures would do but little hurt.

Another evil or inconvenience I see there, the snow in winter did lie very long upon the ground.

But I understand that all the parts of Christendom were troubled with a cold winter so well as we. Yet would I ask any man what hurt snow doeth? The husbandman will say that corn is the better for it. And I hope cattle may be as well fed in the house there as in England, Scotland, and other countries, and he is but an ill husband that cannot find employments for his servants within doors for that time. As for wives and children if they be wise they will keep themselves close by a good fire, and for men they will have no occasion to ride to fairs or markets, sizes or sessions, only hawks and hounds will not then be useful.

Yet let me tell you that it is still almost Christmas before there be any winter there, so that the cold time doth not continue long.

And by all reason that country should be hotter than England, being many degrees farther from the north pole.

And thus according to my poor understanding I have given you the best information I can of the people and country, commodities and discommodities. Now give me leave to oppose myself against the man beforementioned, and others, who speaks against the country and plantations in those parts, and to set down such objections as I have heard them make, and my answers, and afterward let wisdom judge: for my desire is, that the saddle may be set on the right horse, and the ass may be rid, and the knave punished either for discouraging or encouraging too much, whosoever he be.

Certain objections and answers, with sufficient proofs how it may be exceeding profitable to the Commonwealth, and all planters and adventurers.

They say the country is good for nothing but to starve so many people as comes in it.

It is granted that some have been starved to death, and others have hardly escaped, but where was the fault, in the country or in themselves. That the country is as I have said, I can bring one hundred men to justify it; but if men be neither industrious nor provident, they may starve in the best place of the world.

About two years since one Mr. Weston sent over about fifty persons to plant, with little provision; when they came there, they neither applied themselves to planting of corn nor taking of fish, more than for their present use, but went about to build castles in the air, and making of forts neglecting the plentiful time of fishing. When winter came their forts would not keep out hunger, and they having no provision beforehand, and wanting both powder and shot to kill deer and fowl, many were starved to death, and the rest hardly escaped. There are four of his men which escaped, now at my plantation, who have related unto me the whole business.

Again, this last year there went over divers at one time, and to one place, with too little provision; some of them are dead, yet I cannot hear of any that were merely starved, except one whose name was Chapman, a Londoner, and whether he was starved or no is uncertain; but if her were, God's just judgment did appear. For this man (as I am told by an honest man who came from London with him) brought at the least eighty pounds' worth of provision, and no more but himself and two servants, which was sufficient for at the least eighteen months, if it had been well used. And yet in five months after his arrival in New England he died miserably.

Let me tell you a strange thing of this man; (I have it but by relation from one of his companions) he payed for his passage, and his mens', and provision, so that he needed not to have spent any thing until his arrival in New England, yet would he at Plymouth, (where the ship stayed too long for him and others,) spend seven or eight pound a week in wine, tobacco, and whores, and for the maintaining of this expense he daily fetched his provision from aboard, and sold it at a low rate. And when they were at sea, his tobacco being spent, he gave usually sixpence for a pipe; he gave also a suit of clothes, valued to be worth fifty shillings, for so much tobacco as was not worth half a crown. Nay, at last, as his comrade told me, he was glad to become servant to one of his servants. Then his master told him, that if he would work he would allow him one biscuit cake a day, if not he should have but half a cake. He made choice of half a cake, without work; and so a base, lazy fellow made a lamentable end. Where was the fault now, in the men or in the country?

Another objection which I have met with is this: That there is nothing got or saved by sending men over to plant; neither is it beneficial either to private men, either adventurer or planter, or good for the commonwealth.

For answer hereunto, first for matter of profit, it is well known to all the merchants of the west country, who have left almost all other trade but this, and yet is grown rich thereby.

Secondly, for the commonwealth consider these things: 1. The great complaint that hath for a long time been made in England, that our land is overburthened with people, and that there is no employment for our men so that it is likely they must either starve, steal, or prove mutinous. And whether plantations be a means to help this inconvenience or no, I desire to know?

It hath been likewise said unto me, that it benefits the commonwealth nothing at all to send men over with provision of clothes, victuals, and continual supplies.

To that I say, let such men, as you send thither to plant, have provision as Chapman had for eighteen months, and if after, they cannot live of themselves, and be beneficial either to the commonwealth or to themselves, let them die Chapman's death.

Again plantations may be beneficial to the commonwealth, by the enlargement of his Majesty's dominions.

Again by the increase of shipping, (which is the strength of a nation,) and that without wasting of our timber, which is a commodity that I fear England will find the want of before many years pass over; for if timber go to decay as now it doth, we shall scarce have any to build, or repair ships or houses. Again, tell me whether it would be beneficial to the commonwealth to have all our idle persons kept to work, and our populous nation disburthened, and yet to have them ready to serve our king and country upon all occasions.

Lastly, tell me whether it would be beneficial to the commonwealth to have all poor people maintained out of those arts. And every parish freed from their weekly payments to the poor, which if I do [not] make to appear, then let me be accounted an unworthy fellow. But first let me set down another objection, which seems to be of great force, and yet in my conceit is like the rest, shallow, and that is this.

If, say they, there be so many plantations, there will be no room in the country for such ships as do come yearly to make voyages, and by this means ships shall lie still and decay, mariners and fishermen shall want employment, and so all will be out of frame if ever we shall have wars. And therefore, howsoever it may be beneficial to some few persons, yet it will be hurtful to the commonwealth. And consequently all such as have any hand in such businesses are evil members in the commonwealth.

I answer, that if these things were thoroughly examined by his Majesty, the parliament, or council-table, it would plainly appear, that the most of them which keep such ado against plantations, are the greatest enemies to the public good, and that their show of care for the commonwealth is nothing but a color, for the more cleanly concealing of their unknown profits. It will also appear that plantations are for the public good, and by that means there shall be more and better cheap ships built and employed, more mariners and fishermen kept to work than now there are, and more people partakers of the benefit than now there doth.

Which I prove thus: first, there may be timber had to build ships, and ground for corn and keeping of all for little or nothing.

Secondly, there may be more men trained up in fishing than now there is, whose trade is decayed in England, and they ready to starve for want of employments.

Thirdly, there may be twice so much fish taken every year as now there is. For ships that go to make voyages, seldom or never keep their boats at sea above two months or ten weeks for making their voyage, and I dare maintain that there is fish enough to be taken, seven months in the year, if men be there ready to take all opportunities.

Fourthly, the more fish that is taken, the more ships there must be for the transportation of it.

Fifthly, whereas now none doth take the benefit, but a few merchants; not all the merchants in the land, no not one of a thousand;

By plantations, not only all the merchants in the land, but all the people in the land may partake thereof.

And now to shew you how the profit may arise.

Sheweth how by adventuring of a hundred pounds, more or less, a man may profit so much every year, for twenty years or longer, without any more charge than at the first.

I must confess I have studied no other art a long time but the mysteries of New England's trade, and I hope at last, I have attained to the understanding of the secrets of it, which I think the fishermen are sorry for; but it shall be no longer concealed, for that I think every good subject is bound to prefer the public before his own private good.

First, therefore, I will shew you the charge which every merchant is at yearly in sending their ships to fish there, and so near as I can the profit they make of such voyages. Then we will see the charge which planters must be at, in sending men over to stay there, and the profit they are likely to make, and so by comparing the one with the other, we shall see which is the better and more profitable course.

A ship of two hundred ton commonly doth carry in those voyages fifty men; these men are at no charge but twenty shillings a man towards their victuals, neither have they any wages; but in lieu thereof, they have one third part of all the fish and train.

Another third part there is allowed the owners of the ship for their fraught, and the other third part is allowed for the victual, salt, nets, hooks, lines and other implements for taking and making the fish.

The charge of victualling (which is usually for nine months,) the salt, &c., doth commonly amount to about eight hundred pounds; and for that they have (as I said one third part of the fish,) which is near sixty-seven ton, the ship being laden, which will make thirteen hundred and forty quintals, (at the market). Sometimes when they come to a good market they sell their fish for forty-four rials a quintal, and so to thirty-six rials, which is the least, but say they have forty, one time with another, and at that rate one-third of the ships' lading doth yield thirteen hundred and forty pounds, which they have for disbursing of eight hundred pounds nine months.

Now take notice that they are but eight or ten weeks in taking all their fish, and about one month longer in making it fit to be shipped.

Which being considered, then say that such men as are sent over to plant, have twelve months provision, which will amount to one thousand and sixty-six pounds, thirteen shillings four pence; these men stay in the country, and do take the benefit both of the first and last fishing season, and all other opportunities, the fishing continuing good at the least seven months in the year, though not all at one time; now I hope you will grant that they are as likely to take two ships lading as the other one, which if they do, one third thereof at the same rate will amount to two thousand six hundred and eighty pounds; the charge you are at being deducted, the profit is one thousand and nineteen pounds, six shillings, eight pence. Now tell me seriously, which is the more profitable course?

Again consider, that in all likelihood this fish is to be taken in five months, then have you seven months more to employ your men in the country every year, about building of ships, cleaving of pipe-staves, or any other thing, and will that be worth nothing?

Truly this I will say, send men over but with eighteen months' provision, and cattle, and corn to plant, and other necessaries, and they shall afford you thus much profit yearly, without ever putting you to more charge, if God bless them with health, and you, from losses, (and I never heard of any great loss by adventuring thither) and that you be fitted with good and understanding men to oversee the business, who is able to direct them.

Sheweth how every parish may be freed of their weekly payments to the poor, by the profits which may be fetched thence with certain objections against the things contained in this and the former chapter: with answers thereunto.

And thus have I shewed you what hopes there is of profit by plantations, yet have I shewed you no other means to raise it, but by fish and timber. I would not have you say there is nothing else in the country to make any benefit of; for I assure you it is well known to myself, and others who have been there, that there are divers other good things there to be had; but I do not love to speak of all at one time, but to reserve some to stop the mouths of such prating coxcombs as will never be satisfied with any reason, but will always cavil, though to little purpose.

And methinks I hear some such people buzzing in some other objections, and bidding me stay, and not fish before the net, for there are many lets, as these. There are many ships go that make not so good voyages as I speak of: for they are so long beaten in their passage, or on the coast, that the best of the fishing is past before they be there.

To that I answer, I speak not what every ship doth, but what some do, and all others may do, if they be in the country to take all opportunites.

2. Object. That it is not possible to make plantations so public a business, as that it should redound to the benefit of all the king's subjects. And again that there will never be so much money raised as to establish such plantations, for that most men in this age respects their own profit one hundred times more

than the public good; and their hearts are so glued to the world, that you shall as soon hang them as draw anything from them, though it be to never so charitable a use. And if it should be by way of commandment, it would be a grievance not to be endured.

But I would ask such men whether they be so void of charity, as that they will not do themselves good, because some others shall have some by it also? And whether they will be grieved at a man for shewing of them how, by the disbursing of twenty shillings, they shall have twenty shillings a year, for seven, ten or twenty years, and perhaps for ever.

My desire is not that any should be compelled, only this I could wish that every parish would adventure so much as they pay weekly to the relief of the poor (which is not great matter) and so every shire by itself would send over men to plant. And if after eighteen months they shall not yearly return so much profits continually as will keep their poor and ease their purses, (provided always, as I said before, that they send such men as are fit, and that the justices of every shire be careful to appoint such a man to be their captain and director as is honest, and of good understanding, and that God bless them from losses,) will I be contented to suffer death.

And yet let me tell you, that if it should please God, that once in seven years a ship should be cast away (which is more than hath been usual, for I dare say, that for every ship that is cast away in those voyages, there is one hundred which cometh safe) yet it is but that year's profit lost, and perhaps not half.

Another objection may be this, that all men are not fishermen, and that it is not so easy a thing to take fish, as I make it.

To that I answer, that take a survey of all the men that goeth in these voyages, and there shall not be found one-third of them that are merely fishermen, and no other trades.

Nay I know many ship-companies that have amongst them house carpenters, masons, smiths, tailors, shoemakers, and such like, and indeed it is most fit that they should be such: And I saw by experience, that divers who were never at sea before this

year, proved very good fishermen; but I could wish that ever a
fifth part of a company be fishermen, and the rest will quickly
be trained up, and made skilful.

I would to God that some one shire or more would begin
this godly and profitable course. For certainly, God hath created
all for the use of man, and nothing hath he created in vain.

And if we will endure poverty in England wilfully, and
suffer so good a country as this is to lie waste, I am persuaded we
are guilty of a grievous sin against God, and shall never be able
to answer it.

I could also wish, that the lords both spirtual and temporal,
the knights and others to whom God hath given abundance of
these outward things, would (for the honor of God, the comfort
of the poor of our land) join together, and by a voluntary
contribution raise a sum of money, and employ it this way; and
that the profits might go to the maintaining of poor children,
and training them up in this course, by which they may be kept
from begging and stealing.

Contains certain directions for all private persons that intend to go into New England to plant.

Next unto this I could wish that every private man that hath a desire this way, would consider these things which I will here set down, before he go too far, lest he deprive himself of the profit I have showed may be had, and be one of those that repent when it is too late, and so bring misery upon himself, and scandalize the country, as others have done.

1. That it is a country where none can live except he either labor himself, or be able to keep others to labor for him.

2. If a man have a wife and many small children, not to come there, except for every three loiterers he have one worker; which if he have, he may make a shift to live and not starve.

3. If a man have but as many good laborers as loiterers, he shall live much better there than in any place I know.

4. If all be laborers and no children, then let him not fear but to do more good there in seven years than in England in twenty.

5. Let no man go without eighteen months' provision, so shall he take the benefit of two seasons before his provision be spent.

6. Let as many plant together as may be, for you will find that very comfortable, profitable and secure.

Finis.

A GUIDE TO SOURCES
On Maine in the
Age of Discovery
By Emerson W. Baker

Maine was the scene of much activity during the age of discovery. The region was visited by some of the more famous figures in early American history, including John Smith, Samuel de Champlain, and Henry Hudson. Even the Plymouth Colonists frequented Maine, to purchase supplies from the English fishermen, and fur pelts from the native Indians. Maine also saw some of the first attempts at European settlement in North America. In 1604 the French attempted a settlement at the mouth of the St. Croix River, only to abandon the site the next year. Three years later English settlers began a colony at the mouth of the Kennebec River, but the Popham (or Sagadahoc) Colony lasted only one winter. While the St. Croix and Popham ventures were short-lived failures, they comprise some of the first steps toward the colonization of North America.

The initial years of exploration and settlement mark an exciting and important period in Maine's history. During this era the French and English explorers and settlers first came in contact with each other, and with Maine's Indians. The first interactions between these groups had direct implications for the development of Maine and the Maritime Provinces during the colonial period. In many ways, Maine was a very different place over three hundred years ago, and it is only by learning of its origins that we can understand the region today. For instance, the Maine Indian land claims settlement of the 1970s was only the latest chapter in over four hundred years of often turbulent relations between the Indian and European populations of the region.

Necessity has forced this guide to center on the period between 1525 and 1675, a more strictly defined time frame for the discovery period. In 1525 Verazzano sailed the coast of Maine, and the account of his voyage is the earliest written account of an explorer in Maine. In 1675 hostilities broke out between the English and Indian populations of Maine. The conflict, generally referred to as King Philip's War in Maine, brought to an end the first phase of English settlement in the region. Some items pertaining to both earlier and later times are also included, as they contain valuable insights into the period. For example, prehistoric archaeology has provided many important details about the ancestors of the Maine Indians of the seventeenth century. Likewise, some of the best information on Indian-European relations in Maine appears in the accounts and documents relating to King William's War (1689-1697).

This bibliography is not meant to be an exhaustive compendium of all references to early Maine. Instead it provides the reader with an overview of the best and most accessible sources on "The Land of Norumbega: Maine in the Age of Discovery." In particular this guide includes the collections of the Maine Historical Society Library in Portland, although several works are included which are not in the Society's collections. The quest for works on early Maine has already been made easier by the existence of a series of detailed bibliographical guides on the history of Maine. These guides, published in the 1970s by the Maine Historical Society, cover a wide range of topics and time periods in our history. Two of these guides in particular should be used in conjunction with this work: Roger Ray's *Indians of Maine and the Atlantic Provinces: A Bibliographic Guide*, and Charles Clark's *Maine during the Colonial Period: A Bibliographic Guide*.

I. General Works

The following bibliographies contain many important works which are beyond the scope of this essay. The works by Clark and Ray are examples from a series of bibliographies on different eras and aspects of Maine history published by the Maine Historical Society.

Clark, Charles E. *Maine during the Colonial Period: A Bibliographic Guide.* Portland: Maine Historical Society, 1974.

Nelson, Eunice. *The Wabanaki: An Annotated Bibliography.* Cambridge: American Friends Service Committee, 1982.

Ray, Roger B., ed. *Indians of Maine and the Atlantic Provinces: A Bibliographic Guide.* Portland: Maine Historical Society, 1977.

Spiess, Arthur. "A Bibliography of Maine Prehistory through 1981." *Maine Archaeological Society Bulletin* XXII, No. 1 (1982): 28-36.

Quinn, David B. *Sources for the Ethnography of Northeastern North America to 1611.* National Museum of Man Mercury Series, Canadian Ethnology Service, Paper No. 76. Ottawa: National Museum of Man, 1981.

Williamson, Joseph. *A Bibliography of the State of Maine.* Portland: The Thurston Print, 1896.
This two volume work, the "grandfather" of Maine bibliographies, contains references to many hundreds of publications on Maine published up to 1891. An invaluable resource.

There are many good publications on the age of discovery and settlement in the northeast. While these works may speak only briefly about the settlement of Maine, they provide a general overview of the era, and put the Maine experience in a North American perspective.

Axtell, James. *The European and the Indian: Essays in the Ethnohistory of Colonial North America.* New York: Oxford University Press, 1981.

Axtell, James. *The Invasion Within.* New York: Oxford University Press, 1985.
Includes discussion of missionary efforts in Maine.

Bailey, Alfred G. *The Conflict of European and Eastern Algonkian Cultures, 1504-1700.* 2nd. ed. Toronto: University of Toronto Press, 1969.

Cronon, William. *Changes in the Land: Indians, Colonists, and the Ecology of New England.* New York: Hill and Wang, 1983.
An important analysis of the landscape of colonial New England and its peoples.

Cressy, David. *Coming Over: Migration and Communication between England and New England in the Seventeenth Century.* New York: Cambridge University Press, 1987.

Jennings, Francis. *The Invasion of America: Indians, Colonialism, and the Cant of Conquest.* Chapel Hill: University of North Carolina Press, 1975.

McManis, Douglas R. *Colonial New England: A Historical Geography.* New York: Oxford University Press, 1975.

Morison, Samuel E. *The European Discovery of America: The Northern Voyages.* New York, Oxford University Press, 1971.

Quinn, David B. *North America from Earliest Discovery to European Settlements.* New York: Harper & Row, 1977.

Salisbury, Neal. *Manitou and Providence.* New York: Oxford University Press, 1982. Contains interpretations on Indian-European relations in early Maine.

Trigger, Bruce, ed. *Handbook of North American Indians.* XV. Washington, D.C.: The Smithsonian Institution, 1978. Includes a series of articles on each of the tribes of Maine and surrounding areas. An important reference work.

Trudel, Marcel. *The Beginnings of New France, 1524-1663.* Toronto: McClelland and Stewart Limited, 1973.

Vaughan, Alden. *Puritan Frontier: Puritans and Indians, 1620-1675.* 2nd. ed. Boston: Little, Brown and Co., 1979.

MAINE

The first two histories published on Maine both focus on the age of exploration and settlement. James Sullivan's *History of the District of Maine* (1795) is riddled with inaccuracies, but can be interesting reading. Much more reliable is William Williamson's *History of Maine* (1832). While there are some inaccuracies in Williamson, the book holds up well considering it is now over 150 years old. Williamson discusses early Maine in intricate detail, devoting over 600 pages to describe Maine before 1700.

In addition to general histories of Maine, serial publications provide many articles on the topic. One of the richest sources for Maine in the Age of Exploration and Discovery is the Collections of the Maine Historical Society. The Collections, published between 1865 and 1906, include numerous articles on early Maine, as well as transcriptions of primary sources. Many of these have withstood the test of time, particularly the articles by James P. Baxter, Henry O. Thayer, Henry Burrage and Charles Banks. Other articles are of lesser value, but all are important building blocks in the development of our modern-day understanding of early Maine.

Useful articles are scattered throughout several other periodicals, including *Sprague's Journal of Maine History* (1913-1925), and the *Maine Historical and Genealogical Recorder* (1884-1894). While a few of the articles in these and other journals have been individually listed in this bibliography, the reader is directed to these serials for other papers.

Collections of the Maine Historical Society. Portland: Published by the Society, 1865-1906.

Maine Historical and Genealogical Recorder. Portland: S.M. Watson, 1884-1894.

Sprague's Journal of Maine History. Dover-Foxcroft: Sprague's Journal of Maine History, Inc., 1913-1925.

Sullivan, James. *History of the District of Maine.* 1795. Reprint, Portland, Maine: Maine Historical Society, 1978.

Williamson, William D. *History of the State of Maine.* Hallowell, Maine: Glazier and Masters, 1832.

II. Published Primary Sources

Throughout the generations, numerous people have put forward the claim that Maine was visited by Europeans in precolumbian times. Some historians have concluded that Maine was the "Vinland" described in Norse sagas, which was visited by Norse sailors in the ninth and tenth centuries. Other scholars, such as Barry Fell, have made even more incredible claims, suggesting possible visits by ancient Phoenicians, or other early cultures.

Currently no historical or archaeological data exists which supports such hypotheses. Several rune stones and runic inscriptions "discovered" across the state have been examined by experts, and all determined to be either natural phenomena or elaborate fakes. Out of dozens of archaeological excavations which have taken place throughout the region, the only evidence to suggest early European visits to Maine is a Norse coin of the ninth century, discovered at the site of a prehistoric Indian village on Blue Hill Bay. However, this is an isolated Norse find among thousands of native American artifacts. Archaeologists do not believe that the Norse visited Maine. Instead, they posit that the coin reached Maine via an extensive Indian trade network, active throughout the Gulf of Maine and the Maritime Provinces of Canada.

Archaeologists have discovered that in about the year 1000 the Norse did establish a short-lived colony at L'Anse aux Meadow, at the northern tip of Newfoundland. This settlement is apparently the Vinland described in the Norse sagas. It is most likely that the Norse Penny was made into a piece of jewelry and traded from this settlement down the coast to Blue Hill Bay. It would be another five hundred years before Europeans explored Maine.

While Verazzano visited the coast of Maine in 1525, and a report was published of his voyage, few other explorers reached Maine in the sixteenth century. Reconnaissance of the region began in earnest at the turn of the seventeenth-century. Fortunately, narratives survive for many of these early voyages. In 1602 Bartholomew Gosnold explored the coast of New England, and the accounts of the voyage written by John Brereton and Gabriel Archer provide an interesting glimpse of the first English exploration of Maine. A follow up voyage was made by Martin Pring the following year, and a brief narrative appears for this voyage as well. Soon afterwards, in 1604, the French, led by the Sieur de Monts, established a colony on Dochet Island, in the mouth of the St. Croix River. The settlement lasted only a year, before moving north to Port Royal, Nova Scotia. However, the explorations of de Monts' assistant, Samuel de Champlain, have left us a detailed record of the coast of Maine and its native peoples at the turn of the seventeenth century.

Even as the French moved toward Port Royal, the English were preparing for settlement in Maine. The 1605 Waymouth expedition reconnoitered the mid-coastal region of Maine, examining locations for a proposed settlement. James Rosier, a gentleman on the voyage, published a report of the expedition soon after his return to England.

Two years after the Waymouth expedition, the Sagadahoc or Popham Colony began its brief existence at the mouth of the Kennebec River. Fortunately Henry Thayer, the meticulous historian of the Kennebec River, long ago gathered the extensive primary documents on the colony and published these in *The Sagadahoc Colony*. In 1930 Charles Banks published his article "New Documents Relating to the Popham Expedition, 1607," adding several items which had been previously overlooked by Thayer and earlier researchers.

Despite the failure of the Popham Colony, the English continued to visit the coast of Maine. Perhaps the best known of these trips was by Captain John Smith, of Virginia fame, who mapped the coast of Maine and New England in 1614. Smith's important narrative has been published in many forms.

One of the most significant exploration narratives of Maine is Christopher Levett's "A Voyage into New England begun in 1623 and ended in 1624." Levett extensively explored southern and mid-coastal Maine, and lived on Casco Bay for about a year. He became fast friends with the Indians of Maine, and traded with them. Levett's account was first published in the *Collections of the Maine Historical Society*, and was reprinted with notes by James P. Baxter in 1893. An authoritative edition of Levett, annotated by Roger Howell Jr., can be found in this volume.

Two volumes in particular should be noted, as they bring together many of the exploration narratives. George Winship's *Sailors' Narratives of Voyages Along the New England Coast, 1524-1624* (1905) include the accounts of virtually all known voyages to New England from Verazzano to Levett. Almost as valuable is Henry Burrage's *Early English and French Voyages Chiefly from Hakluyt* (1906), which contains many exploration accounts, including the voyages of Jacques Cartier, and the 1607 *Relation of a Voyage to Sagadahoc*.

Arber, Edward, ed. *Travels and Works of Captain John Smith*. 2 vols. Westminster, England: Archibald Constable and Co., 1895. Smith visited the coast of Maine in 1616.

Archer, Gabriel. "The Relation of Captain Gosnold's Voyage to the North Part of Virginia." Massachusetts Historical Society *Collections* 3d Ser.,VIII (1843): 72-79.

Banks, Charles E. "New Documents relating to the Popham Expedition." *Proceedings of the American Antiquarian Society*, 1929 (1930).

Baxter, James P., ed. *Sir Ferdinando Gorges and His Province of Maine* 3 vols. Boston: The Prince Society, 1890.

Baxter, James P., ed. *Christopher Levett of York, the Pioneer Colonist of Casco Bay*. Portland: The Gorges Society, 1893.

Biggar, Henry Percival, ed. *The Works of Samuel de Champlain*. 6 vols. Toronto: The Champlain Society, 1922-36.

Burrage, Henry S., ed. *Rosier's Relation of Waymouth's Voyage to the Coast of Maine, 1605*. Portland: The Gorges Society, 1887.

Burrage, Henry S., ed. *Early English and French Voyages Chiefly from Hakluyt*. New York: Charles Scribner's Sons, 1906.

Collections of the Maine Historical Society, Second Series: *Documentary History of the State of Maine.* 24 vols. Portland: The Maine Historical Society, 1869-1916. This set is the single most important source of primary materials on colonial Maine.

Lescarbot, Marc. *The History of New France.* 1618. Edited by W.L. Grant. 3 vols. Toronto: The Champlain Society, 1907-14. Lescarbot was a member of the St. Croix Colony.

Lescarbot, Marc. "The Defeat of the Armouchiquois Savages by Chief Membertou and his Savage Allies," trans. Thomas Goetz. In *Papers of the Sixth Algonquian Conference,* 1974, Edited by William Cowan. National Museum of Man Mercury Series, Canadian Ethnology Paper 23. Ottawa: National Museums of Canada, 1975.

Morton, Thomas. *The New English Canaan or New Canaan: Containing an Abstract of New England Composed in Three Books.* 1637. Edited by Charles Adams. Boston: The Prince Society, 1883.

Otis, Charles P., ed. *Voyages of Samuel de Champlain.* 2 vols. Boston: The Prince Society, 1880.

Purchas, Samuel. *Hakluytus Posthumus or Purchas His Pilgrimes.* Vol. XIX. New York: The Macmillan Co., 1906.

"Reports of the Country Sir Humphrey Gilbert Goes to Discover." David B. Quinn, ed. *The Voyages and Colonizing Enterprises of Sir Humphrey Gilbert.* Vol. II. London: The Hakluyt Society, 1940.

Quinn, David B. "The Voyage of Etienne Bellenger to the Maritimes in 1583." *Canadian Historical Review* XLIII (1962): 328-43. Bellenger may have visited Penobscot Bay.

Thayer, Henry O., ed. *The Sagadahoc Colony.* Portland, Maine: The Gorges Society, 1892. Includes the relation of the Sagadahoc Colony's voyage.

Thwaites, Reuben G., ed. *The Jesuit Relations and Allied Documents.* 73 vols. Cleveland: Burrows Brothers, 1896-1901. The Jesuits were among the best observers of the Indians of North America, and some of the first explorers of Maine.

Winship, George P., ed. *Sailors' Narratives of Voyages Along the New England Coast, 1524-1624.* 1905. Reprint. New York: Burt Franklin, 1968. Includes almost all of the surviving explorer accounts from this time.

SETTLEMENT

The student of Maine's settlement is indeed fortunate that the bulk of the early surviving records has been transcribed and published. Since the late nineteenth century the Maine Historical Society has taken the lead in publishing these primary sources. *The Province and Court Records of Maine*, a six volume set, includes all the surviving court records from 1636-1727. The companion 18 volume set, *York Deeds*, includes land transactions for Maine from 1636-1737.

Many other papers, drawn from the Massachusetts archives and other official repositories in New England and Europe, are published in the twenty-four volume set, the *Documentary History of the State of Maine*. This monumental work, primarily edited by James Phinney Baxter, is the most encompassing primary source for the study of early Maine. While most of the *Documentary* series is official correspondence and papers, volume three, The Trelawney Papers, provides a more personal look at life in early Maine. The papers are the correspondence of John Winter, the agent for the fishing station on Richmond Island. His letters provide details of the day to day life of people on the coast of Maine.

The Letters of Thomas Gorges, edited by Robert Moody, is a set of eighty letters written by the Lieutenant Governor of Maine which are contemporary with the Trelawney Papers. Gorges wrote of the many trials he faced in York as he tried to organize the government of the Province of Maine. While Gorges and Winter are full of personal insights, only John Josselyn published an account of his experiences in early Maine. Josselyn's" An Account of Two Voyages to New England" summarizes his experiences of two trips to Maine in 1636 and between 1668 and 1672. Josselyn describes the native Indians and the English settlers, as well as the flora and fauna of Maine.

Some of the most interesting sources on early Maine are the histories of King Philip's War in Maine, and King William's War. William Hubbard's *The History of the Indian Wars in New England* (1677) is one of the best sources not only for King

Philip's War, but also for examining Anglo-Indian relations. Cotton Mather's *Magnalia Christi Americana* provides similar information for King William's War. Although both Hubbard and Mather are clearly biased in favor of the English, these accounts are worthy of close attention.

While many of the documents and accounts of early Maine have been published, several repositories still contain sizable collections of unpublished materials which the serious scholar will want to consult. The largest collection of early Maine materials is located in the Massachusetts Archives, in Boston. The Public Archives of Canada, in Ottawa, holds copies of documents from French Archives relating to New France, including Acadia. In state, the Maine State Archives, the Maine State Library, and the Maine Historical Society all contain important materials. Many other repositories contain small document collections. Those interested in locating specific manuscripts should consult Elizabeth Ring's authoritative work, *A Reference List of Manuscripts Relating to the History of Maine.*

Baxter, James P., ed. *Sir Ferdinando Gorges and His Province of Maine.* 3 vols. Boston: The Prince Society, 1890.

Boulton, Nathaniel, ed. *Documents and Records Relating to the Province of New Hampshire.* Vol. I. Concord, N.H.: George E. Jenks, State Printer, 1867.

Bradford, William. *History of Plymouth Plantation, 1620-1647.* 2 Vols. Boston, Houghton Mifflin Company, 1912.
Includes details of the Plymouth Colony's activities in Maine.

Bradford, William. *Of Plymouth Plantation.* ed. by Samuel E. Morison. New York: Alfred A. Knopf, 1952.

Church, Thomas. *The History of Philip's War, Commonly called the Great Indian War, of 1675 and 1676.* Edited by Samuel G. Drake. 2nd ed. Exeter, New Hampshire: J. & B. Williams, 1829.

Collections of the Maine Historical Society, Second Series: *Documentary History of the State of Maine.* 24 vols. Portland: The Maine Historical Society, 1869-1916.
This set is the single most important source of primary materials on colonial Maine.

Denys, Nicholas. *The Description and Natural History of the Coasts of North America (Acadia).* ed. and trans. by William F. Ganong. Toronto: The Champlain Society, 1908.

Hubbard, William. *The History of the Indian Wars in New England*. 1677. Edited by Samuel G. Drake. Roxbury, Mass.: W. Eliot Woodward, 1865. New York: Burt Franklin, 1971.
A detailed account of King Philip's War in Maine.

Josselyn, John. "An Account of Two Voyages to New England."Massachusetts Historical Society, *Collections*, 3d Ser., III (1833). Josselyn visted Maine in 1636 and again between 1668 and 1672. Strong on details about the native flora and fauna.

Libby, Charles T., Robert E. Moody, and Neal W. Allen, Jr. *Province and Court Records of Maine*. 6 vols. Portland: Maine Historical Society, 1928-1975.

Lindholdt, Paul J., ed. *John Josselyn, Colonial Traveler: A Critical Edition of Two Voyages to New England*. Hanover: University Press of New England, 1988.

Mather, Cotton. *Magnalia Christi Americana*. 1701. Edited by Thomas Robbins. Hartford: Silas Andrus & Son, 1853.

Maverick, Samuel. "An Account of New England." *Proceedings of the Massachusetts Historical Society* 2d Ser., I (1885): 231-49.

Moody, Robert E., ed. *The Letters of Thomas Gorges*. Portland: Maine Historical Society, 1978.
Thomas Gorges, Lieutenant Governor of the Province of Maine from 1640-1642, wrote over eighty letters to England, describing his life and activities in the colony.

Ring, Elizabeth, ed. *A Reference List of Manuscripts Relating to the History of Maine, Compiled under the Auspices of the Department of History and Government of the University of Maine with Funds Provided by the Federal Emergency Relief Administration*. 3 vols. University of Maine Studies, 2nd. Ser., No. 45. Orono: University Press, 1938-41.

Shurtleff, Nathaniel B., ed. *Records of the Governor and Company of Massachusetts Bay in New England*. 5 vols. Boston: Press of William White, 1853.

Shurtleff, Nathaniel B., ed. *Records of the Colony of New Plymouth in New England*. 10 vols. in 11 books. Boston: Press of William White, 1855.

Thayer, Henry O., ed. *The Sagadahoc Colony*. Portland, Maine: The Gorges Society, 1892. Includes the relation of the Sagadahoc Colony.

Winthrop, John. *History of New England*. 2 vols. New York: Charles Scribners' Sons, 1908. While Winthrop's history is focused on activities in southern New England, he does occasionally mention affairs in Maine.

York Deeds. 18 vols. Portland: Maine Historical Society, 1887-1911.
A transcription of the deeds from 1636-1737. Before 1760, all of Maine was part of York County.

III. Special Topics

PREHISTORIC ARCHAEOLOGY

Native Americans have a long tradition in Maine. Approximately eleven thousand years ago the first paleoindians ventured North into the region, as the glaciers retreated. Since that time, a series of native cultures have occupied Maine.

Archaeologists have been active in Maine for approximately 100 years; however, the overwhelming majority of professional research in the field has taken place within the past twenty years. This time has seen the growth of a professional community that has taken rapid strides to unravel the mysteries of Maine's prehistoric past. The following list presents only a small sample of some of the more available works on Maine prehistory. In addition to these references, the reader is directed to the *Maine Archaeological Society Bulletin,* which contains a variety of articles on the topic. Many papers on Maine prehistory are also published in *Man in the Northeast.* Arthur Spiess' "A Bibliography of Maine Prehistory through 1981" is a good compilation of sources in Maine prehistory.

Borstel, Christopher L. *Archaeological Investigations at the Young Site, Alton, Maine.* Occasional Publications in Maine Archaeology, 2. Augusta, Maine: Maine Historic Preservation Commission, 1982.

Bourque, Bruce J. and Steven L. Cox. "The Maine State Museum Investigation of the Goddard Site, 1979." *Man in the Northeast* XXII (1981): 3-27. A summary of excavations at a late ceramic period Indian village where a Norse silver penny was discovered.

Bourque, Bruce J. "The Turner Farm Site: A Preliminary Report." *Man in the Northeast* XI (1976): 21-30.

Bourque, Bruce J. "Aboriginal Settlement and Subsistence on the Maine Coast." *Man in the Northeast* VI (1973): 3-20.

Bourque, Bruce J. "Prehistory of the Central Maine Coast." Ph.D. dissertation, Harvard University, 1971.

Cook, David. *Above the Gravel Bar: The Indian Canoe Routes of Maine.* Milo: Published by the Author, 1985.

Cox, Steven L. "The Blue Hill Bay Survey." *Maine Archaeological Society Bulletin* XXIII, No. 2 (1983): 21-30.

Gramley, Richard Michael. *The Vail Site: A Paleo-Indian Encampment in Maine.* Buffalo: Buffalo Society of Natural Sciences, 1982.

Moorehead, Warren K. *Archaeology of Maine.* Andover, Mass.: The Andover Press, 1922.
Modern Maine archaeologists are highly critical of Moorehead's methodologies.

Petersen, James B. and Nathan D. Hamilton. "Early Woodland Ceramic and Perishable Fiber Industries from the Northeast: A Summary and Interpretation." *Annals of Carnegie Museum* LIII, (1984): 413-446.

Ray, Roger. "The Embden, Maine, Petroglyphs." *Maine Historical Society Quarterly* XXVII, No. 1 (1987): 14-23.

Sanger, David. *Discovering Maine's Archaeological Heritage.* Augusta: Maine Historic Preservation Commission, 1979.
A series of articles on different periods in Maine's prehistory, written primarily by Sanger.

Sanger, David. "Passamaquoddy Bay Prehistory: A Summary." *Maine Archaeological Society Bulletin* XI, No. 2 (1971): 14-19.

Snow, Dean. "Rising Sea Level and Prehistoric Cultural Ecology in Northern New England." *American Antiquity* XXXVII No. 2 (1972): 211-21.

Snow, Dean. *The Archaeology of New England.* New York: Academic Press, 1980.
Contains useful basic information, although many archaeologists consider Snow's theories and conclusions to be controversial.

Spiess, Arthur E., Bruce J. Bourque, and Steven L. Cox, "Cultural Compexity in Maritime Cultures: Evidence from Penobscot Bay, Maine." In Nash, Ronald J., ed. *The Evolution of Maritime Cultures on the Northeast and Northwest Coasts of America.* Publication No. 11. Simon Fraser University, 1983.

Spiess, Arthur E., and Mark Hedden. *Kidder Point and Sears Island in Prehistory.* Occasional Publications in Maine Archaeology, 3. Augusta, Maine: Maine Historic Preservation Commission, 1983.

Spiess, Arthur E. "A Bibliography of Maine Prehistory through 1981." *Maine Archaeological Society Bulletin* XXII, No. 1 (1982): 28-36.

Spiess, Arthur E. "A Skeleton in Armor: An Unknown Chapter in Maine Archaeology." *Maine Archaeological Society Bulletin* XXII, No. 1 (1982): 17-24.

Tuck, James A. *Maritime Provinces Prehistory.* Ottawa: National Museums of
Canada, 1984.
The Maritimes were home to many of the same prehistoric cultures as
Maine.

Willoughby, Charles C. *Indian Antiquities of the Kennebec Valley.* Occasional
Publications in Maine Archaeology, 1. Augusta, Maine: Maine Historic
Preservation Commission, 1980.

NATIVE AMERICANS AND THEIR RELATIONS WITH EUROPEANS

In recent years, just as our understanding of Maine prehistory
has grown, so too has interest in the Indians of Maine in
historic times. The interaction between the European and
native populations in Maine is one of the most important
themes of the Age of Discovery. Indian-European relations
include such diverse elements as the fur trade, the land trade,
missionary activities, diplomatic negotiations, and warfare.

The interplay of these forces has always been of interest to
historians. William Williamson gave much attention to the
Indians of Maine in his *History of Maine;* unfortunately, and
uncharacteristically for Williamson, he makes many factual
errors in his discussion of the topic. In the mid nineteenth
century Samuel Drake published his *Book of the Indians* and
edited an edition of Hubbard's *History of the Indian Wars.* While
today's scholars have found some errors in Drake, his work is
still very informative, and quite readable. In the first half of the
twentieth century, Frank Speck dominated the ethnography of
Maine. Speck did extensive fieldwork with the Penobscots and
other tribes throughout North America. He left a huge body of
work, including *Penobscot Man: The Life of a Forest Tribe in Maine.*

In the mid twentieth century, the work of Bernard Hoffman
and Fannie Hardy Eckstorm greatly advanced the study of the
Indians of Maine. Eckstorm's most notable work is her *Indian
Place Names of the Penobscot Valley and the Maine Coast.* Hoffman
challenged Speck's analysis of tribal divisions in early Maine in
his "Souriquois, Etchemin and Kwedish: A Lost Chapter in
American Ethnography," and began a debate which continues
today.

Since the 1970s, a series of scholars have begun to restudy and revise the ethnohistory of Maine. Alvin Morrison, Kenneth Morrison, Gordon Day, Bruce Bourque and others have made significant contributions to furthering our understanding of such issues as tribal divisions, the fur trade, acculturation, and Indian-European relations. Today ethnohistory continues to be one of the most vigorous and fruitful areas of study in Maine history.

Baker, Emerson. "Trouble to the Eastward: The Failure of Anglo-Indian Relations in Early Maine." Ph.D. dissertation, College of William and Mary, 1986.

Baker, Emerson. "John Howland's Howling Wilderness: Myth, Reality and Cushnoc." *The Kennebec Proprietor* III, No. 2 (1986), 4-10.

Bourque Bruce J., and Ruth H. Whitehead. "Tarrentines and the Introduction of European Trade Goods in the Gulf of Maine." *Ethnohistory* XXXII (1986):327-41.

Bourque, Bruce J. "Aboriginal Settlement and Subsistence on the Maine Coast." *Man in the Northeast* VI (1973): 3-20.

Day, Gordon M. *The Identity of the Saint Francis Indians* Ottawa: National Museum of Man Mercury Series, Canadian Ethnology Service, Paper No. 71. Ottawa: National Museum of Man, 1981.

DePaoli, Neill. "The New England Settler's Perception of the Amerindian, 1640-89: A Case Study of the Impact of Conflict and Locale." M.A. thesis, Brown University, 1979.

DePaoli, Neill. "Beaver, Blankets, Liquor and Politics: Pemaquid, Maine's Participation in the Seventeenth- and Eighteenth-Century Anglo-Indian Trade." Paper presented at the annual meeting of the Council for Northeast Historical Archaeology, Ottawa, 1985.

Drake, Samuel G. *The Book of the Indians.* 9th ed. Boston: Benjamin B. Mussey, 1845.

Eckstorm, Fannie Hardy. *Indian Place Names of the Penobscot Valley and the Maine Coast.* Orono, Maine: University of Maine Press, 1941.

Harrington, Faith. "Sea Tenure in Seventeenth-Century New England: Native Americans and Englishmen in the Sphere of Marine Resources, 1600-1630." Ph.D. dissertation, University of California at Berkeley, 1985.

Height, Horatio. "Mogg Heigon—His Life, Death, and its Sequel," *Collections of the Maine Historical Society* 2nd Ser., V (1895): 345-60; 2nd Ser., VI (1896): 256-80.

Hoffman, Bernard G. "Souriquois, Etchemin and Kwedish: A Lost Chapter in American Ethnography." *Ethnohistory* II (1955): 65-87.

Hornbeek, Billee. "An Investigation into the Cause or Causes of the Epidemic which Decimated the Indian Population of New England 1616-1619." *The New Hampshire Archaeologist* XIX (1977): 35-46.

Morrison, Alvin. "Membertou's Raid on the Chouacoet 'Almouchiquois'— The Micmac Sack of Saco in 1607." In *Papers of the Sixth Algonquian Conference,* 1974. Edited by William Cowan, 141-58. National Museum of Man Mercury Series, Canadian Ethnology Paper 23. Ottawa: National Museums of Canada, 1975.

Morrison, Alvin. "Dawnland Decisions: Seventeenth-Century Wabanaki Leaders and their Response to Differential Contact Stimuli in the Overlap Area of New France and New England." Ph.D. dissertation, State University of New York, Buffalo, 1974.

Morrison, Kenneth M. *The Embattled Northeast: The Elusive Ideal of Alliance in Abenaki-Euramerican Relations.* Los Angeles: University of California Press, 1985.

Morrison, Kenneth M. "The Bias of Colonial Law: English Paranoia and the Abenaki Arena of King Philip's War, 1675-1678." *New England Quarterly,* LIII, No. 3 (1980):363-378.

Morrison, Kenneth M. "The People of the Dawn: The Abnaki and their Relations with New England and New France, 1600-1727." Ph.D. dissertation, University of Maine, 1975.

Nelson, Eunice. *The Wabanaki: An Annotated Bibliography.* Cambridge: American Friends Service Committee, 1982.

Prins, Harald, and Bruce Bourque. "Norridgewock: Village Translocation on the New England-Acadian Frontier." *Man in the Northeast* XXXIII (1987):

Prins, Harald. "'The Most Convenientest Place for Trade:' A Discussion of the Kenibec/Cushnoc Controversy." *The Kennebec Proprietor* III, No. I (1986): 4-9.

Ray, Roger B. "Maine Indians' Concept of Land Tenure." *Maine Historical Society Quarterly.* XIII, no. 1 (1973): 28-51.

Roberts, William I., "The Fur Trade of New England in the Seventeenth Century." Ph.D. dissertation, University of Pennsylvania, 1958.

Salisbury, Neal. *Manitou and Providence.* New York: Oxford University Press, 1982.

Sevigny, Pere-Andre. *Les Abenaquis: Habitat et Migrations (17e et 18e siecles).* Montreal: Les Editions Bellarmin, 1976.

Siebert, Frank. "The Identity of the Tarrantines, with an Etymology." *Studies in Linguistics* XXIII (1973): 69-76.

Siebert, Frank. "Review of *Indian Place Names of the Penobscot Valley and the Maine Coast*, by Fannie Hardy Eckstorm." *New England Quarterly* XVI (1943): 505-6.

Snow, Dean. "The Ethnohistoric Baseline of the Eastern Abenaki." *Ethnohistory* XXIII (1976): 291-306.

Spiess, Arthur E., and Bruce D. Spiess. "New England Indian Pandemic of 1616-1622: Cause and Archaeological Implications." *Man in the Northeast* XXXIV (1987): 71-83.

Speck, Frank. *Penobscot Man: The Life of a Forest Tribe in Maine.* Philadelphia: University of Pennsylvania Press, 1940.

Trigger, Bruce, ed. *Handbook of North American Indians.* XV. Washington, D.C.: The Smithsonian Institution, 1978.

Whitehead, Ruth H. *Elitekey: Micmac Material Culture from 1600 AD to Present.* Halifax: The Nova Scotia Museum, 1980.

EXPLORATION & THE POPHAM COLONY

Few modern Maine historians have focused on the Age of Exploration. One of the best locally-produced efforts is Henry Burrage's *The Beginnings of Colonial Maine, 1602-1658.* The most recent interpretation of the exploration of Maine is included in the works of Samuel Eliot Morison and David Beers Quinn, the foremost authorities on the exploration of the North Atlantic.

The short-lived Popham Colony, perhaps the single most important episode in the early exploration of Maine, received great attention by nineteenth-century researchers. While the Popham Colony had been noted by Sullivan, Williamson, and others, in 1862 the Colony took center stage in Maine history. That year marked the dedication ceremonies of the United States Army Fort Popham, located in Phippsburg near the believed site of the 1607 colony. At the dedication ceremonies, sponsored by the Maine Historical Society, Maine scholars argued strongly that the Popham Colony had not been entirely abandoned in 1608. They suggested that a small settlement remained in the area in the 1610s and 1620s. Hence, the

Popham Colony, not Plymouth Colony, was allegedly the first permanent colony in New England.

Not surprisingly, Massachusetts historians took exception to this undocumented claim, and a fierce scholarly debate ensued. Within six years, a total of ninety-eight pamphlets and articles appeared arguing the Popham and Plymouth sides of the debate. Three books bring together many of these arguments. First, in 1862 John A. Poor published *Vindication of the Claims of Sir Ferdinando Gorges*. The next year Edward Ballard, Secretary of the Maine Historical Society, edited a transcript of the dedication ceremonies entitled *Memorial Volume of the Popham Celebration, August 29, 1862*. Finally, 1866 saw the publication of *The Popham Colony; a Discussion of its Historical Claims, with a Bibliography of the Subject*. By the early twentieth century, research in English archives had produced ample evidence to determine that the Popham Colony had indeed been completely abandoned in 1608, and the lengthy debate came to an end.

The late nineteenth and early twentieth century exploration scholarship was dominated by James P. Baxter, Henry O. Thayer, Henry Burrage, and Charles Banks, all meticulous scholars who grounded their research in detailed studies of the existing primary sources. These men published many important articles in various journals. One such journal was volume two of the second series of the *Collections of the Maine Historical Society,* an issue dedicated largely to the topic of exploration. Published in 1906, the volume contains many essays celebrating the tercentenary of the voyages of Martin Pring, George Waymouth, and the settlement of the St. Croix Colony. Baxter, Thayer, and Burrage all contributed to the volume. The most encompassing work on the topic is Henry Burrage's excellent *Beginnings of Colonial Maine, 1602-1658*. Relatively little research has been done on exploration by Maine historians since these early twentieth century efforts. In the 1970s Edwin Churchill did revise one popular misconception of the exploration of Maine in his research on the early fishing industry. Many previous historians had suggested that fishermen had been in Maine long before 1600, possibly even before Columbus "discovered" the new world. However, Churchill found no evidence for such early visits and determined that European fishermen began working on the coast of Maine only in the 1610s. Since little research has been done on the age of exploration by recent Maine scholars, the most current information on the topic can be found in the general works on the discovery of North America by David Quinn and Samuel E. Morison.

Ballard, Edward. *Memorial Volume of the Popham Celebration, August 29, 1862.* Portland: Bailey and Noyes, 1863.

Baxter, James P. "Christopher Levett, the First Owner of Soil in Portland." *Collections of the Maine Historical Society.* Ser. 2, IV (1893):169-185, 301-320.

Bradley, Robert L. "The European Exploration and Settlement of Maine." Unpublished manuscript in possession of the author, 1985.

Burrage, Henry S. *The Beginnings of Colonial Maine, 1602-1658.* Portland: Marks Printing House, 1914.

Churchill, Edwin A. "The Founding of Maine, 1600-1640: A Revisionist Interpretation." *Maine Historical Society Quarterly* XVIII (1978): 21-54.

Folson, George. *Address Delivered on the Site of the Popham Colony, near the Mouth of the Kennebec in New England, before the Maine Historical Society, on the twenty-eight of August, 1863.* Ventnor, Isle of Wight: Fletcher Moore, 1866.

Moody, Robert Earle. "The Maine Frontier, 1607-1763." Ph.D. dissertation, Yale University, 1933.

Morison, Samuel E. *The European Discovery of America: The Northern Voyages.* New York: Oxford University Press, 1971.

Poor, John A. *Vindication of the Claims of Sir Ferdinando Gorges.* New York: D. Appleton and Co., 1862.

The Popham Colony; a Discussion of its Historical Claims, with a Bibliography of the Subject. Boston: J.K. Wiggin and Lunt, 1866.
Includes several opinions in the Popham debate, including Edward Ballard's.

Quinn, David B. *North America from Earliest Discovery to European Settlements.* New York: Harper & Row, 1977.

Salisbury, Neal. *Manitou and Providence.* New York: Oxford University Press, 1982.

Spencer, Wilbur, D. *Pioneers on Maine Rivers.* Baltimore: Genealogical Publishing Co., Inc., 1973 (orig. publ. 1930).

Thayer, Henry O. *The Sagadahoc Colony.* Portland, 1892.

ENGLISH SETTLEMENT

Maine had barely left the colonial period in 1795 when James Sullivan published the first book on the subject, *History of the District of Maine.* Since Sullivan's initial, and often inaccurate efforts, many scholars have turned their talents to under-standing diverse aspects of early Maine's history.

While Sullivan was the first Maine historian, William D. Williamson stands as the most important early scholar of the region. Williamson's two volume *History of the State of Maine* (1832) remains even today as one of the most detailed histories of colonial Maine. Unfortunately, not all of Williamson's con-temporaries held his high standards. Rufus Sewall's *Ancient Dominions of Maine* (1859) unnecessarily shrouded Maine's history in romantic myths of ancient civilizations and pre-columbian explorers inhabiting Maine. What Sewall and others claimed were "Vinland" and "Norumbega" had correctly been identified by Williamson as cellarholes and other physical remains of seventeenth-century Maine.

The late nineteenth and early twentieth centuries were productive times for the historians of colonial Maine. Such major scholars as James P. Baxter, Henry O. Thayer, Charles Libby, Charles Banks, and others were responsible for bringing together our present wealth of primary documents. While these men devoted themselves to gathering data, they also produced some important books and papers. However, the single most important book on early Maine published in this era was written by Henry Burrage. In 1914 the eminent State Historian brought much of this past research and articles together in a major monograph, *The Beginnings of Colonial Maine, 1602-1658.* To this day, Burrage's work remains an important reference book.

Few secondary sources on early Maine appeared in print for over fifty years following *The Beginnings of Colonial Maine.*

While the study of early Maine entered a "dark age," there were several breakthroughs in the 1930s. In 1933 Robert Moody completed his excellent dissertation, "The Maine Frontier, 1607-1763," but it was never published. The 1930s also saw the publication of a most important source, *The Genealogical Dictionary of Maine and New Hampshire*. This huge effort, undertaken by Sybil Noyes, Charles T. Libby, and Walter G. Davis includes references for everyone known to have lived in the two colonies in the seventeenth-century. While strictly speaking a genealogical source, the authors combed New England archives for documents, making the volume a vital reference work for any researcher of the period.

The study of seventeenth-century Maine entered an exciting new era in 1970 with the publication of Charles Clark's *The Eastern Frontier: The Settlement of Northern New England, 1610-1763*. Departing from the traditional political history format, Clark was the first to study Maine and New Hampshire from the perspective of the "new" social history. Subsequent to Clark's work, numerous historians undertook studies of specialized aspects of early Maine. These scholars utilized an array of interdisciplinary approaches to better understand early Maine's social, political, and economic climate. For example, Edwin Churchill drew on community studies as well as climate history in his case study of the early years of the settlement of Casco Bay.

Other historians also found fruitful avenues of research in early Maine studies. Laurel Ulrich, a student of Clark's, explored women's history in *Good Wives: Images and Reality in the Lives of Women in Northern New England, 1650-1750* (1982). John Reid's two monographs examined the political environment of Maine, and its marginal nature as a colony. Reid provided an important comparison between the Province of Maine and its northern neighbors, Acadia and New Scotland.

Other researchers utilized historical archaeology to provide many of the details of daily life in Maine which escape the documentary record. Historical archaeology in Maine truly began in the 1960s, when excavations commenced at Pemaquid under the direction of Helen Camp. Excavations continued at Pemaquid until the early 1980s, with Camp and Robert Bradley overseeing work on the colonial settlement and its fortifications. Few objects survive from Maine in the age of discovery except for those excavated from archaeological sites. Colonial Pemaquid State Park, one of the largest repositories of these artifacts, includes a museum where the public may view Maine's material past.

Most of Maine's historical archaeologists have been trained at Pemaquid or under Alaric Faulkner at the University of Maine. Faulkner has been active in Maine since the late 1970s, working principally on the English fishing station on Damariscove Island and the French fortress of Pentagoet (in present-day Castine).

Baker, Emerson W. *The Clarke & Lake Company: The Historical Archaeology of A Seventeenth-Century Maine Settlement.* Occasional Publications in Maine Archaeology, 4. Augusta, Maine: Maine Historic Preservation Commission, 1985.

Baker, William A. *A Maritime History of Bath, Maine and the Kennebec Region.* Bath, Maine: Marine Research Society of Bath, 1973.

Banks, Charles E. "The Pirate of Pemaquid." *Maine Historical and Genealogical Recorder* I, (1884): 57-61.

Banks, Charles E. *History of York, Maine.* 2 vols. Boston: The Calkins Press, 1931.

Bradstreet, Theodore E. "Agry's Point Status Report." *Maine Archaeological Society Bulletin* XXI, No. 1 (1981): 13-27.

Bradley, Robert L. *Maine's First Buildings, The Architecture of Settlement, 1604-1700.* Augusta, Maine: Maine Historic Preservation Commission, 1978.

Burrage, Henry S. *The Beginnings of Colonial Maine, 1602-1658.* Portland: Marks Printing House, 1914.

Camp, Helen, *Archaeological Excavations at Pemaquid, Maine 1965-1974.* Augusta, Maine: The Maine State Museum, 1975.

Camp, Helen. "Makers' Marks on White Clay Pipes from Colonial Pemaquid." *Maine Archaeological Society Bulletin* XXII, No. 2 (1982): 24-40.

Carroll, Charles E. *The Timber Economy of Puritan New England.* Providence, R.I.: Brown University Press, 1973.

Cass, Edward. "Settlement on the Kennebec, 1600-1650." M.A. thesis, University of Maine, 1970.

Churchill, Edwin A. "A Most Ordinary Lot of Men: The Fishermen at Richmond Island, Maine in the Early Seventeenth Century." *New England Quarterly* LVII, No. 2 (1984): 184-204.

Churchill, Edwin A. "The Founding of Maine, 1600-1640: A Revisionist Interpretation." *Maine Historical Society Quarterly* XVIII (1978): 21-54.

Churchill, Edwin A. "Too Great the Challenge: The Birth and Death of Falmouth, Maine, 1624-1676." Ph.D. dissertation, University of Maine, 1979.

Clark, Charles E. *The Eastern Frontier: The Settlement of Northern New England, 1610-1763.* New York: Alfred A. Knopf, 1970.

Clark, Charles, E. "The Founding of Maine, 1600-1640: A Comment." *Maine Historical Society Quarterly* XVIII (1978): 55-62.

Elwell, Eben. "A New Look at Early Pilgrim Activity at 'Kenibec.'" *The Mayflower Quarterly* XLVII, No. 2 (1981): 57-65.

Faulkner, Alaric. "Archaeology of the Cod Fishery." *Historical Archaeology* XIX, No. 2 (1985): 57-86.

Folsom, George. *History of Saco and Biddeford.* 1830. Reprint. Portland, Maine: Maine Historical Society, 1975.

Griffin, Carl R., III, and Alaric Faulkner, "Coming of Age on Damariscove Island." *Northeast Folklore* XXXI, 1980.

Harrington, Faith. "Sea Tenure in Seventeenth-Century New England: Native Americans and Englishmen in the Sphere of Marine Resources, 1600-1630." Ph.D. dissertation, University of California at Berkeley, 1985.

Leamon, James S. "Historians in the Woods: Historical Archaeology at the Clarke & Lake Site, Arrowsic, Maine." In *New England Historical Archaeology.* Edited by Peter Benes, 16-23. Dublin Seminar for New England Folklife, Annual Proceedings, II. Boston: Boston University Press, 1978.

Moody, Robert Earle. "The Maine Frontier, 1607-1763." Ph.D. dissertation, Yale University, 1933.

Moorehead, Warren K. "The Ancient Remains at Pemaquid, Maine: Some Observations." *Old Time New England,* XIV (1924): 131-42.

Noyes, Sybil, Charles T. Libby, and Walter G. Davis. *Genealogical Dictionary of Maine and New Hampshire.* Baltimore: Genealogical Publishing Company, 1979 (orig. publ. 1928-1939).

Ranlet, Philip. "The Lord of Misrule: Thomas Morton of Merrymount." *New England Historical and Genealogical Register* CXXXIV (1980): 283-88.

Reid, John G. *Acadia, Maine and New Scotland: Marginal Colonies in the Seventeenth Century.* Toronto: University of Toronto Press, 1981.

Reid, John G. *Maine, Charles II, and Massachusetts: Governmental Relations in Early Northern New England.* Portland, Maine: Maine Historical Society, 1977.

Sewall, Rufus. *Ancient Dominions of Maine.* Bath, Maine: Elisha Clark and Company, 1859.

Spencer, Wilbur, D. *Pioneers on Maine Rivers.* Baltimore: Genealogical Publishing Co., Inc., 1973 (orig. publ. 1930).

Sullivan, James. *History of the District of Maine.* 1795. Reprint, Portland, Maine: Maine Historical Society, 1978.

Ulrich, Laurel T. *Good Wives: Images and Reality in the Lives of Women in Northern New England, 1650-1750.* New York:Alfred A. Knopf, 1982.

Williamson, William D. *History of the State of Maine.* Hallowell, Maine: Glazier and Masters, 1832.

Yentsch, Anne. "Expressions of Cultural Variation in Seventeenth-Century Maine and Massachusetts. Albert E. Ward, ed. *Archaeological Perspectives on American History.* Contributions to Anthropological Studies, III. Alburquerque, N.M.: Center for Anthropological Studies, 1984, 117-131.

THE FRENCH

The French claimed and occupied northern Maine for much of the seventeenth century, establishing a presence in 1604, with the St. Croix colony. Unfortunately, the French in Maine have never received as much attention from historians as have the English. In the nineteenth-century few efforts were made to understand the French presence in Maine, other than those of George Wheeler.

Wheeler was the local historian in Castine, the center of French activity in seventeenth-century Maine. While the French made some brief attempts at settlement and missionary activity in Maine after the failure of the St. Croix Colony, it was not until Pentagoet was occupied in 1635 that the French established a permanent base in Maine. The stone fortress of Pentagoet was destroyed by Dutch raiders in 1674, however the French presence in the region was soon reestablished by Baron Saint-

Castin. The Baron became a firm ally of the Indians of the region, and he and his family played important roles in the frontier wars of the late seventeenth and early eighteenth centuries.

Aside from the work of Wheeler and several other turn-of-the-century historical and archaeological efforts focused on Pentagoet, relatively little research was done on Acadian Maine until the late 1960s. In 1968 Andrew Clark published *Acadia,* an historical geography of the region. Archaeological excavations of the St. Croix Colony site were carried out by Jacob Gruber in 1968 and 1969; unfortunately, little has been published on this site. Clark's and Gruber's efforts were followed closely by George Rawlyk's *Nova Scotia's Massachusetts: A Study of Massachusetts-Nova Scotia Relations, 1630 to 1784* (1973).

Several recent works have provided knowledge about the social and political atmosphere of Acadian Maine. John Reid's *Acadia, Maine and New Scotland: Marginal Colonies in the Seventeenth Century* (1981) is a detailed study in comparative history which examines the lack of success of three neighboring colonies. Reid's book was published the same year that Alaric and Gretchen Faulkner began their archaeological investigation of Fort Pentagoet. Four seasons of excavation, combined with painstaking research, have produced spectacular results. The Faulkners' publications, including a series of articles and the major monograph, *The French at Pentagoet, 1635-1674: An Archaeological Portrait of the Acadian Frontier,* have finally begun to give the Acadian presence its proper place in early Maine history.

Burrage, Henry S. *The Beginnings of Colonial Maine, 1602-1658.* Portland: Marks Printing House, 1914.

Clark, Andrew Hill. *Acadia.* Madison: University of Wisconsin Press, 1968.

Cotter, John L. "Les Premiers etablissements francais en Acadie: Sainte-Croix et Port Royal." *Dossiers de L'archeologie,* no. 27, 1978.

Faulkner, Alaric. "Pentagoet: A First Look at Seventeenth-Century Acadian Maine." Northeast Historical Archaeology X (1981): 51-57.

Faulkner, Alaric, and Gretchen F. Faulkner. "The Settlement of Acadian Maine in Archaeological Perspective." *Northeast Historical Archaeology* XIV (1981): 1-20.

Faulkner, Alaric, and Gretchen F. Faulkner. *The French at Pentagoet, 1635-1674: An Archaeological Portrait of the Acadian Frontier.* Augusta: The Maine Historic Preservation Commission, 1987.

Leach, Douglas. "The Question of French Involvement in King Philip's War." *Publications of the Colonial Society of Massachusetts.* XXXVIII (1953): 414-21.

MacDonald, M.A. *Fortune and LaTour: The Civil War in Acadia.* Toronto: Methuen, 1983.

Parkman, Francis. *Pioneers of France in the New World.* Boston: Little, Brown and Company, 1865.
While Parkman's historical analyses and interpretations are outdated, his powerful writing style makes his narratives highly readable.

Rawlyk, George A. *Nova Scotia's Massachusetts: A Study of Massachusetts-Nova Scotia Relations, 1630 to 1784.* Montreal: McGill-Queen's University, 1973.

Reid, John G. Acadia, *Maine and New Scotland: Marginal Colonies in the Seventeenth Century.* Toronto: University of Toronto Press, 1981.

Wheeler, George A. *History of Castine, Penobscot and Brooksville.* Bangor: Burr and Robinson, 1875.

Wheeler, George A. "Fort Pentagoet and the French Occupation of Castine." *Collections of the Maine Historical Society.* Ser. 2, IV (1893): 113-23.

Williamson, William D. *History of the State of Maine.* Hallowell, Maine: Glazier and Masters, 1832.